Dad Died, then Mom

SIBLINGS' SPIRITUAL & INSPIRATIONAL MEMOIR AS CAREGIVERS

by Malia Arries

A wholly owned subsidiary of TBN

Dad Died, Then Mom

Trilogy Christian Publishers A Wholly Owned Subsidiary of Trinity Broadcasting Network

2442 Michelle Drive Tustin, CA 92780

Manufactured in the United States of America

10 9 8 7 6 5 4 3 2 1

Library of Congress Cataloging-in-Publication Data is available.

ISBN: 978-1-68556-685-2

E-ISBN: 978-1-68556-686-9

Mom and Dad (Bill and Inez Arries), wedding photo

June 21, 1947

Children or grandchildren "should learn as their first duty to show loyalty to the family and to repay what they owe to their parents and grandparents; for this God approves" (1 Timothy 5:4, NEB).

Acknowledgments

I had just lain down on the sofa to take an afternoon nap when, for some unexplainable reason, visions with words began popping into my mind describing the night Dad died. It was so overwhelming I needed to get up and start typing them into a document. And this was over six years after both Dad and Mom had died! I noted to call my sister, Franchion, to ask her if I could borrow *The Notebook*. It was the type of diary we kept during Dad's and later Mom's time under hospice care while remaining in their home. I envisioned using that as a source for this writing.

There are so many who deserve recognition for contributing during that time, including the following:

Thank you, Meals on Wheels, for all the prepared and delivered meals, as well as the added thoughtful surprises.

Maureen Anderson and Trenton Berg of Anderson Funeral Home in Augusta, Wisconsin, you are gifted people in your profession. Your dad/grandfather would be incredibly proud of how you two are continuing the reputation he earned.

Grace Lutheran Church in Augusta, Wisconsin, you were Mom and Dad's church home since way before I was born. Thank you, staff and members, Pastor Cal Siegel, and Pastor Jonathan Wessel, for your comforting actions and words.

St. Joseph Hospice in Chippewa Falls, Wisconsin, deserves more gratitude than I can express. You were with us sometimes daily caring for Dad, then Mom. The names of those who helped us care for Dad and Mom include the supervisor Charlotte, the aides Juanita, Heather, Beth, Faye, and Karen, the nurses Sara, Cindy, Barb, Rita, Deb, Billie, Debbie, and John, and the social worker Diane.

The many friends who never stopped calling and/or visiting, along with Mom and Dad, we all appreciated you so much. Joyce Richards, thank you for your *lifelong*, cherished friendship with Mom and Dad.

Joe Haak, I will never forget your contribution to Dad's funeral. Thank you.

All of Mom and Dad's family members are immensely loved. Thank you for being a part of our family. Rocky Arries, Kay Connors, Uncle Alvin Erdman, and Aunt Aubrey Wittren, special hugs for you.

Marvel and Steve Barka, Franchion and Keith LeMere, Shonnie and Art Brazeau, and Bill and Linda Arries, there is absolutely no way of expressing how fortunate I feel having you as siblings. Marvel, Franchion, Shonnie, and Bill, you guys contributed to 4/5 of the notebook! Thank you! I love you all!

My husband, Darrell Shelby, you were there, living with me at Mom and Dad's many days and nights. I have no idea how many errands you ran, things you repaired, or help you provided...all without complaint. And then making meals, doing dishes, and taking care of Ellie and Shelby while I was writing this. Thank you with all my love!

Mom and Dad, thank you for my momentous childhood. Thank you for your devoted guidance and friendship as an adult. Thank you for showing me how to die so gracefully and so beautifully.

I love you! I miss you! I look forward to dancing with both of you in heaven!

Table of Contents

Part 1: Dad

Dad's About to Die

The streetlight found its way into the room around the edges of Mom's heavy drapes to outline objects, my sister Franchion, and my dad. A lingering smell of rhubarb custard pies Mom had made over the years now competed with odors of medicines, cleaning supplies, and body wipes. Fresh lilacs I had picked earlier that day and placed by Dad's hospital bed offered a glimpse and scent of spring.

I had always loved hearing their grandfather clock, musically announcing the quarter hours and then banging out the full hours. But on that night, I was consciously and unconsciously focused only on the sound of Dad's breathing.

The living room floor carpeting felt cushy enough, so I was sleeping on that with a pillow and a blanket next to Dad's bed. My sister's choice was his big, plush recliner. We both wanted to be near Dad. Franchion was unable to sleep, but I had drifted off until Dad's breathing changed.

One: Summer And Autumn 2012

Unchartered Territory

My husband, Darrell, and I had gone to a local "Northwoods" Wisconsin supper club for dinner and were enjoying the wait for our food when Mom called. Her usual vibrant and full-of-life happy voice was sounding strained with uncertainty and fright. Dad was in the hospital. His kidneys were shutting down. She wanted us to come home. Our food was quickly and carefully packed for us to take, but my empty stomach was now filled with an alarming dread.

It had only been a few days earlier I was polka dancing with Dad. That day was incredibly festive since we were celebrating Mom and Dad's sixty-fifth wedding anniversary with not only an extensive number of family members but also with a wonderful group of friends. The celebration was held at a lovely venue with food, etc., and moreover, with Mom and Dad's favorite old-time polka band providing the entertainment. Mom and Dad were glowing that day! They were so overjoyed when even my non-dancing siblings and their spouses with the rest of the siblings and spouses joined them on the dancefloor to honor their incredible marriage journey.

Mom and Dad (front), Steve, Marvel, Franchion,
Shonnie, Malia, Darrell (middle, left to right),
Bill, Linda, Keith, Art (back, left to right)

My siblings are Marvel, married to Steve; Franchion, married to Keith; Shonnie, married to Art; and Bill, married to Linda. As we gathered around Dad and Mom at the hospital before Dad was taken in for surgery to drain his kidneys, there was an overwhelming silent realization that we were about to experience a change in our lives, that we were facing the fact that our parents' time with us on earth will come to an end. And what does that mean? What happens then?

I wondered what Mom was thinking and feeling. She and Dad were so beautifully bonded with a love we were fortunate to take for granted as kids and to admire as adults. *Had Mom and Dad talked about what would happen when one of them died and the other was left to live alone?*

We prayed for a successful outcome to Dad's surgery and expressed our love for each other. The surgery went fine. However, healing from it was complicated since tubes were left in to allow Dad's kidneys to drain, bypassing his bladder. None of us had any idea what that would involve. His caregivers were incredible at teaching us how to flush the tubes and keep the skin around the area where they were inserted clean to prevent infection. I offered to stay with Mom and Dad to help after he left the hospital. Our journey into unchartered territory had begun.

Disaster Treatment

Dad would also need to start dialysis three times each week since his kidneys were barely functioning. He came to absolutely dread those treatments. He referred to them as his "disaster treatments." We did our best to encourage him to continue. Along with Mom, at least one or two of us stayed at Dad's bedside to help support him during each procedure.

This continued until it became so frustrating for Dad that he started talking about not doing them anymore. We arranged to meet with his nephrologist to discuss Dad's options. Dad outright asked the doctor what would happen if he stopped doing the dialysis. The doctor explained that his kidneys would not be able to function on their own and that Dad would die within a week or two. Dad asked what dying would be like by doing that. The doctor gently told him it would not be a difficult death.

Then Dad looked at all of us and asked us what we thought. I don't remember Mom saying anything; I'm quite certain they had already discussed it. We were in tears. Some of us told him that he should continue with the dialysis. Dad was quiet and listening. I didn't know what to say, and then I remembered what Dad would say many times to us when we asked him for advice, "Use your own best judgment." So that's what I said to him. Dad slowly turned to face the doctor and said, "That's what I want to do." To clarify, the doctor asked him if he had decided to stop the dialysis, and Dad said yes.

The doctor referred Dad to St. Joseph Hospice situated at Chippewa Falls, Wisconsin, to help us deal with the reality we were facing that Dad's diagnosis was terminal. There would be no more treatment procedures or medications; now, medications would be prescribed and procedures done only to keep Dad as comfortable as possible.

Leaving the doctor's office on that day, July 13, 2012, was a surreal experience. *Was Dad really going to die? That didn't seem possible!*

Absolutely incredible hospice caregivers were assigned to give instruction and guidance on how to help him, Mom, and all of us navigate this journey to the end of Dad's life. Mom appeared strong and encouraging; she was always "there" like every other day had been with Dad throughout their marriage.

Rocky's Visit

Dad's nephew, Rocky (Dad's brother's son), planned a surprise trip to see Dad. Rocky flew from Albuquerque to Minneapolis, and Franchion and I drove there to pick him up. Dad knew something was up and was absolutely delighted when he saw Rocky walk into the room! The visit gave Dad a huge boost. He and Rocky joked with each other like they always had when they were together.

Rocky, Dad, Mom, and Sugarfoot

Aunt Aubrey (Dad's sister) visited Mom and Dad often, and when she saw her nephew, Rocky, she was overjoyed too. There was a lot of laughing and reliving of great times!

Aunt Aubrey and Rocky

Miraculously Dad's kidneys began to function on their own! I wonder if it had anything to do with the joy Rocky's visit had brought. After Rocky left, Mom and Dad were comfortable staying by themselves in their home for days at a time since hospice caregivers, my siblings and I, friends, and other family members were stopping in regularly.

Dad spent most of his time in his recliner, including sleeping at night. The recliner was situated so that he could see out the windows and also what was going on in the house. Mom slept in their bedroom.

Distributing Possessions

Dad wanted to give each of us things of his while he was still with us. It was important to him to let us know the history of items and to make sure they went to the person he wanted to have them.

Bill recalled helping Dad to the garage because Dad wanted to go through his tools for Bill to pick out the ones he wanted. Mostly Bill remembered Dad telling him about where and when he got them. Bill said, "It was a good time just to talk and be with Dad." Dad also wanted to buy Bill a new gun; Bill told him he didn't need one. On another occasion, Bill mentioned that Dad knew how much he liked a pair of his red cufflinks, so Dad gave them to him. It meant a lot that Dad personally handed his possessions to each of us; every item was a special gift with a story to remember him by.

He gave away just about everything, including his boots and shoes. On a beautiful Sunday afternoon, Dad felt well enough that he wanted to attend a dance, as he and Mom had done so many times in their years together. We got him dressed up but then realized he had given away all his shoes; he didn't have any shoes to wear! Since he was going to be staying in his wheelchair visiting with friends and not dancing, he said his hospital socks would be just fine to wear.

Dad and Sugarfoot

Over the years, Mom and Dad had saved many coins, numerous jars and cans filled with them! One day when all of us were at their house, Mom and Dad asked us to divide them up. As we sat around the table, each container was dumped in the middle. Dad just held his head in his hands when yet another container would be brought out; he didn't think they had that many!

We separated them equally. The odd number left and the unusual or special coins we divided by playing a game. Mom wrote down a number between one and twenty, then each of us said a number between one and twenty; whoever was closest got the coin. Dad was laughing, watching us because we were having so much fun with the game. As I recall, Shonnie came out like a bandit! She even won a vintage coffee can we had emptied, choosing the number eleven, which Mom had written down! There were so many containers filled with only pennies that we simply took them to the bank coin-counting machine; I'm sure there were collectible pennies included. The people at the bank waiting on us said it was the most pennies they had ever seen come in at one time!

Mom and Dad

How Do You Say Goodbye?

I remember talking with Dad one night after Mom had gone to bed. He had chosen to sit in his blue rocking chair that evening. I was sitting on the floor in front of him. I told him I was really struggling because I didn't know how I was going to say goodbye to him.

We were both weeping. Between sobs, Dad said, "The hardest thing for me is to leave you kids." Then he said that we didn't need to worry about it, that it would work itself out the way it's meant to happen.

I think he and Mom had talked about leaving each other often. Though still incredibly painful for them to part, I believe they accepted it as temporary and focused more on being together in heaven.

Two: November and December 2012

Thanksgiving and Christmas

What a blessing it was to be able to spend one more Thanksgiving with both Mom and Dad! My husband Darrell and I had Thanksgiving dinner at our house near Rhinelander, Wisconsin. As Dad came through the front door, he stopped and looked up at the deer mount that Darrell and I had hung there. It was from a deer Dad had shot while hunting. Nobody said anything while he remained focused on it for a few minutes. I'm sure he was reminiscing on a part of his life that he had enjoyed so much.

Along with their stunning tree, Mom and Dad had always put up many strings of lights and incredibly festive decorations for Christmas. Nothing was mentioned about decorating as Christmas 2012 was approaching. While Darrell stayed with Dad, I drove Mom to Eau Claire to shop for something new. She chose a couple of pretty hanging decorations and a lovely fully decorated and pre-lit tabletop Christmas tree. We placed the tree in front of a window in the living room where Dad could see it. He thought it was beautiful.

Christmas Eve that year was a special gathering of the nuclear family and spouses, a very intimate and memorable time with Mom and Dad.

I remember Dad watching as I was setting the table. He

commented on how I could possibly make that many trips from the hutch to the table! It was such a pleasure for me, with Mom's suggestions, to make the table special. The seating arrangement (with our spouses) was how we had sat around the table when we were young kids growing up on the farm.

Rather than recite our usual dinner prayer, we held hands and sang a traditional Christian hymn. Truly it was a very blessed last Christmas for us to be together.

The above photo was taken on Christmas Eve 2012.
Dad (far right, then counter-clockwise around the table),
Malia, Darrell, Art, Keith, Franchion, Mom, Bill, Linda,
Shonnie (Steve took the photo), and Marvel.

Three: Winter 2012 and Spring 2013

Establishing a Routine

By the end of February 2012, it was clear Dad was feeling more uncomfortable and that one of us would need to be with Mom and Dad 24/7. We *wanted* to be with them. We *wanted* to help! We established a routine by setting up a flexible weekly schedule taking turns being with them. Marvel or Shonnie usually covered Saturdays and Sundays, Franchion Mondays and Tuesdays, I covered Wednesdays and Thursdays, and Bill covered Fridays. All of us became comfortable flushing the tubes that drained Dad's kidneys out his back, giving him his medications, etc.

It was more challenging to become comfortable with Dad's intimate care needs, his sponge baths. The first time I bathed Dad, we began by talking about it being hard for both of us, then we agreed to "just get it done!" Darrell installed a bidet which helped tremendously. The social worker, Diane, also asked Dad how he felt about it when Franchion was there. Franchion said Dad looked at her and asked, "Are you kids okay with it?" After Franchion responded that we were, Dad turned back to Diane and affirmed, "I think we're doing okay."

It was becoming increasingly difficult to care for Dad in his recliner. Hospice had a hospital bed prepared to be delivered whenever he was ready for it. We talked to Dad about how it would be easier for us to care for him and that he would likely be more comfortable too. Dad was understandably hesitant but then agreed to it after we assured him the bed would be set up in the exact same place as his recliner was in the living room.

Dad never lost his incredible sense of humor. It took two of us to grab the bottom sheet on each side of Dad to boost him back up from the constant sliding down in the hospital bed. Only my husband, Darrell, was there once to help me. I told Darrell that on "three," we would boost Dad back to the head of the bed. Darrell was not familiar with how much boost was needed and gave quite a bit more than usual. Dad responded by saying, "Osseo's looking pretty good." Osseo is the town located about ten miles in the direction we slid him.

Dad's appetite was nearly impossible to manage. Even though he would feel hungry, nothing tasted right, and he just couldn't eat. It was troublesome to see him losing weight. He would often ask for just half an egg for breakfast. One day I noticed a pair of mourning doves acting strangely outside Mom and Dad's window. Finally, the female laid an egg right there on the ground by the house! Both doves flew away and didn't come back to the egg. After some time had passed, I walked out and picked it up. I brought it into the house and showed it to Dad. I said, "Look, Dad, an egg just your size for breakfast!" He laughed.

The Eagle

Dad was sitting raised up in his bed, casually visiting with Darrell. I was in the kitchen when I heard Dad shout, "Did you see that?"

Darrell and I, at about the same time, replied, "What?" Dad excitedly recounted how he watched this huge bald eagle fly from across the street directly at the window he was facing, then just before hitting the glass, it swooped up and over the house!

Because Darrell had his back to the window and I was busy washing dishes, we hadn't seen it. Dad was definitely amazed and delighted with that experience.

The Notebook

Since Dad's medications and dosages were frequently changing, we began to keep a notebook on March 30, 2013, so everyone knew what medications to give and when to give them. We also added how/what Dad was eating, how things were going for him and Mom, and whatever else we felt like sharing. It was always lying open to the current day on Mom and Dad's breakfast counter. The hospice caregivers appreciated it because after they would arrive, they could read our notes and feel completely caught up to date on everything. Even though the notebook appeared to be a bit chaotic, it became the invaluable source for this writing.

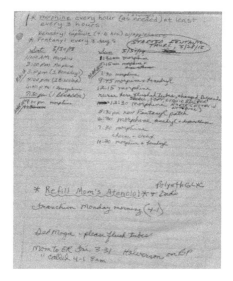

The first page of the notebook

Diapers and Flops

Poor Dad, he endured so much pain from horrible bowel problems. He needed to wear adult diapers 24/7, and we were the ones who changed them. Dad repeated the old worldly phrase, "Once a man, twice a baby." It became comical as we thought back. Shonnie divulged, "And remember the times we had to change his? I was laughing and gagging at the same time."

Poor Franchion, she was the one who was usually staying with Dad during his worst bouts of diarrhea. As she added, "Oh man, he was so constipated until everything let loose. There were some major blowouts!"

Marvel and Shonnie were at Mom and Dad's, and Dad was sitting up on the couch. He became too weak to walk the few feet back to his bed. Shonnie described what happened: "He was a dead weight and just like a rag doll. Marvel took one side, I took the other, we picked him up, told him to put his arms around my neck. We spun him around, kinda did a little dance, barely made it to the bed, and flopped him down."

Franchion and I took Mom and Dad to a doctor's appointment; Dad was in his wheelchair. We had help from the hospice nurse to get him out of the house, down the back stairs, and into the car. We had set up the ramp to the front door in order to get Dad back into the house when we returned.

However, we hadn't measured the front door to get his wheelchair through it. The door was not wide enough! Dad was completely unable to stand, and Franchion and I could not both be in the doorway to help each other lift Dad through it. I told Dad to put his arms around my neck. I took a deep breath and hoisted him up. I stumbled backward into the living room to where I felt the arm of the sofa to rest on. Dad started to slip through my arms before Franchion could help me. I grabbed Dad tightly and threw us both toward his bed, praying Dad would land in it. Thankfully, he did.

Beginning Signs of Dying

Loss of appetite was something we understood as an early sign of the dying process, so we were very aware of it with Dad. Franchion noted on April 2, 2013, "[smiley face] Appetite for Dad so much better and tastes good." It was exciting to report when he ate well.

The first unusual comment Dad made was on the next morning, the third of April, when he said, "There's always someone behind me." Darrell and I noticed that he kept trying to look behind and over the head of his bed. Dad seemed to be trying to see who it was. There was nobody there that Darrell and I could see.

Dad was beginning to feel more pain by the fifth of April. In addition to a fentanyl patch, we were advised by his hospice nurse to increase his morphine dose to every hour if needed. Perhaps it was due to these medications that Dad was beginning to experience unusual things, or maybe he was beginning to experience his transition from this life to his afterlife. We kept track of it all in the notebook.

Shonnie was staying with Mom and Dad when she noted that Dad was "Daydreaming @ Fall Creek bank." Mom and Dad had banked in Fall Creek, Wisconsin, for many years, and that is where Dad did his banking for his feed business, "Bill's Feed & Farm Supply."

On April 11, Marvel wrote in the notebook that Dad "says he feels split down the middle, two different bodies." This was the first time he started talking about his two bodies. This perplexed and fascinated us as well as sadly reminded us that Dad's on a journey that will separate him from us.

Together Through Dying Process

The notebook entries allowed us to live through Dad's dying experience with each other. I always looked forward to reading what everyone else wrote to not only stay caught up with the routine things but moreover to share the unusual or special things. It was great to always feel so connected!

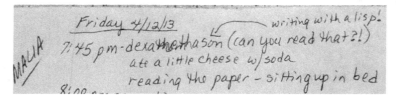

Friends continued to visit. Mom and Dad absolutely loved going to dances, playing cards, and just spending time with others. On April 17, Franchion noted that a couple visited between 2:30 and 4:00, "Really enjoyed, but took a lot of energy." The next day she wrote, "Dad so very tired, weak, and out of it. Said he's a 'total wreck.' Wanted to sit up but can hardly open eyes or talk, doesn't know what he wants."

One of Dad's favorite caregivers, who he had not seen for a while, was going to be checking him on April 22. When Dad found out, he wanted her to see him up in his wheelchair. He did so well while she was there! He enjoyed seeing her tremendously!

On the twenty-third of April, Franchion shared, "Dad was having a good day. He was sitting up in his bed reading the newspaper while Mom was sitting in her recliner. Mom said, 'Franchion, I have a job you can do. You can cut my toenails. They're like horse hooves.' Dad laughed and said, 'That would be good, then I wouldn't have to do it anymore, but watch out 'cause she kicks!'" Dad loved to tease Mom because her feet were very ticklish.

Pasquale

One of the last days Dad was taken to Eau Claire for palliative treatment, we stopped at his favorite restaurant for chicken dumpling soup. Dad liked their soup, and he really liked a waiter there who Dad had affectionately nicknamed "Pasquale."

They had enjoyed kidding each other back and forth over the past few years. So much fun for them! When I went into the restaurant, he was working and recognized me. He asked about Dad. I told him Dad was very ill and that he was dying.

When I added that Dad was outside in the car, the waiter immediately followed me out of the restaurant, where Dad was sitting in the passenger seat. "Pasquale" opened the car door and gave Dad an incredibly long-lasting and emotional hug. He told Dad that he would pray for him. Tears were flowing; what a personal moment between the two of them, knowing they would not be seeing each other again in this world.

Caring for Mom

Mom had health concerns, and adding more stress with Dad's condition caused her blood pressure to rise to 209/139 on April 23. Marvel took her to the ER in Eau Claire while her husband, Steve, stayed with Dad. Mom was instructed to increase the dosage on one of her medicines until she saw her doctor and to monitor her blood pressure three times a day.

Her blood pressure stabilized. We made sure she got all of her prescriptions and took her to her doctor's appointments. Franchion entered in the notebook on May 1, 2013, "Mom, nothing to eat or drink after 10:00 p.m. 'til labs @ 10:00 a.m. on Thursday. May take morning meds with sips of water." We did what we could to support Mom, and we certainly continued to monitor her blood pressure.

Four: May 2013

More Dreams

Dad started having more dreams where he would talk. The morning of May 1, 2013, Franchion noted, "Another night of dreams and talking." The following morning at 7:45 a.m., I jotted in the notebook, "Kinda awake, thirsty, drank a couple sips water, asked for coffee, didn't really have any, fell asleep. *So tired.* Talked (whispered) about a long driveway/sidewalk. During the night, he talked about seeing light in a building/shed. Wondering what it was."

After waking one morning, Dad talked about a dream from the previous night where two people came to visit him. He thought one was a doctor because he wore a white coat, and the other was a female nurse. Dad asked the man if he was a doctor; he said no. The woman also replied no when Dad asked her if she was a nurse. Dad described the woman as being dressed in dark clothes with her hair in a bun.

Went for a Drive

Franchion and Keith came up on the afternoon of May 4, so Bill could go home to get a little sleep before going to work early the next morning. Something Mom and Dad always had tremendously enjoyed was going for drives. Dad loved his cars! So Franchion and Keith took them out for a tour that day. As Franchion noted, "Went cruising, Osseo, Fairchild, Coon Fork." They had a wonderful afternoon driving by where Dad had grown up, the farm where Mom and Dad raised us, and other memorable places.

Perhaps that drive reminded Dad to resolve a concern he had regarding leaving Mom. When they went anywhere together, it had been Dad who (almost) always did the driving. As Keith recalled:

We were all gathered on a Sunday afternoon. Dad called me over and said he was worried that Mom had not been driving much and wanted her to get comfortable driving the new car. He wanted to know that she could get around and take care of herself without him.

I then floated the idea to the group that Mom should go out for a drive. It was not a popular idea. Mom had experienced some health issues, and the medication she was on made driving not safe. Pretty much everyone thought it was a terrible idea, myself included.

My problem was that Dad had squeezed my hand and asked me to please make sure that Mom could drive the car if she needed to. Intellectually I wanted to say no; emotionally, I had to say yes.

We ended up going for a drive. Mom did great and really enjoyed herself. Afterward, both Mom and Dad felt better knowing Mom could drive herself if need be. I was thrilled that Mom had done so well and that I was not excommunicated from the family.

Our Song for Dad

We began thinking about Dad's funeral. The directors, Maureen Anderson and Trenton Berg of Anderson Funeral Home in Augusta, Wisconsin, would be guiding us through the process.

I had always liked using a particular song when teaching the dance known as Bolero. However, for the last few years, it was becoming more difficult to use because the lyrics triggered an emotional response I didn't want to feel. I knew then it would be a good choice for Dad's funeral.

When I asked my siblings about using the song, they all agreed. We also thought Dad would like knowing it was going to be played at his funeral. On May 9, 2013, Darrell and I played a video of the song so Dad and Mom could hear the music as well as read the lyrics.

We were all wiping tears from our eyes, and I wondered if maybe it had been a mistake showing it to them. It was painful facing the reality that the next time we viewed it, Dad would not be with us. How moving when he asked to watch it again!

Earlier on that day, Dad had given Mom her Mother's Day gift. (Mother's Day was actually on May 12 that year.) A while back, Dad noticed how Mom liked a pair of shoes the hospice nurse wore. He asked us to find a pair so he could surprise Mom for Mother's Day with her own. Mom was thrilled, and Dad was beaming!

That evening at 8:00, when Shonnie was staying with Mom and Dad, she wrote, "Dad says his stomach hurts and feels like he's split down the middle. He asked if he looks like he's at the end of his rope."

The next day Bill came and was excited that Dad had some beer with him! It was a good day for Dad. Bill noted that "Dad wanted to sit up in bed with his legs over side (felt good). Mom cut Dad's hair. I tried to shave him (not very good job)."

On May 11, Darrell and I were staying with Mom and Dad. That night at 7:00, I jotted down what Dad had said, "Talked about the farm, [his] Uncle Rowin, John Shong [neighbor], Arden and Dale [his cousins], Thompson Valley Church (never knew about that church), Methodist Pastor would pick up Dad and Aubrey and drive them to that church for Sunday school. The church was across Walker Road from Hank's [Dad's mother's friend] farm (on that corner)."

Big Change

Monday, May 13, 2013, a big change was noted in Dad's condition. He didn't want any pills or morphine. He was very nauseous all day. The next morning, he was feeling the same. Shonnie called the hospice nurse regarding his nausea.

Franchion arrived that morning at 11:00. Dad woke up enough to tell Shonnie to "be a good girl" when she needed to leave. Franchion wrote in the notebook what was said early in the afternoon: "'Heaven is a beautiful place,' looking forward to seeing his dad and Grandma [his mother] and Brooks [his brother], and Hank [his mother's friend]. I told him he would be there to greet all of us when we came. He said, 'I guess that's right.' Dad asked for water and said he loved all of us. Asked about everyone that he is so blessed to have us all. He is in no pain right now."

Later that same day, Aunt Aubrey, Bill and Linda, and Marvel and Steve came. At 3:45, Franchion noted, "We started talking to Dad, and he woke up, noticed all of us here. He gets emotional when we talk about how much we love him and will miss him—tears flow (from all of us). Aubrey is talking to Dad about seeing their dad and mom. Will (Bill) took off from work and is working on Dad's garden tractor tire with Steve." Dad fell asleep.

He woke again when Darrell and I, along with our dog, Libby, arrived at about 4:00. By 8:15, it was just Mom, Franchion, Darrell, and I with Dad. Franchion noted, "He woke up tearful, expressed our feelings again for each other. Dad was very alert. There was a pause, and then he asked, 'What field is this?' I asked what kind of field, and he said, 'Where people are buried.' I said, 'Thompson Valley' [that's the cemetery where Mom and Dad have their plots], and he acknowledged that and went to sleep."

May 15, 2013

Dad woke up at 4:30 that morning, looked at me, and said, "Hi, Malia." He went right back to sleep until waking up very alert at 6:00. He ate a bite of cookies with a little juice and a sip of coffee. Then he said, "Thought yesterday...last night...was going to be it." Dad was very emotional but said he felt good. He sat up with his legs over the side of the bed.

When Mom got up and came into the room, Dad's eyes brightened. Mom told him she had been thinking about him all night. Dad asked her if it was bad; she replied by shaking her head yes. Dad's eyes twinkled with a wink, and he smiled because he knew she hadn't heard him!

I asked Dad if he'd had any dreams during the night. This is how Franchion noted his reply, "There was a funeral, and all of us kids were there and two pastors."

Around noon that day, Dad began to feel more restless. For the first time, he stated that he "just wants this to be over" and "wondering how long this can last." The hospice aide arrived about that time to give Dad his bath and shave; Franchion added in the notebook, "So Will doesn't have to. Yay! [smiley face]"

By 5:20 that afternoon, Dad was very restless again. As I wrote, "Feels so uneasy, legs over the side sitting up, then leaning back, then laying back down. Again he asked about his condition; wants it over."

May 16, 2013

At 6:00 that morning, I noted, "He wonders what today will bring, wants it over. Said, 'I thought the other day was gonna be the end; something ain't right... I guess it doesn't matter what we think; it's what *He* thinks.' Dad doesn't have any pain; he said, 'Thank goodness for that.'"

Then I added in the notebook, "Dad dreamt there was a machine he was riding on with other people, on the streets of a city, and 'the machine never breaks down.'"

At about 10:15, the hospice nurse arrived to check on Dad. She asked him how the aide had done yesterday with his bath and shave. Dad responded, "She must've done alright. I got wet." We all laughed. Dad asked the nurse if there was any pill he could take to "go to sleep." She said, "No, ya gotta ride it out." Then he told her, "I feel split down the middle. One side wants to do something different than the other."

Bill and Linda's New Home

After the nurse left, Dad really wanted to go to see Bill and Linda's new home to surprise them. Darrell had gone there earlier to help Bill with his lawn sprinkler system. As the hospice aide and I were struggling, trying to get Dad into the car, Darrell arrived back at Mom and Dad's. Thank goodness, since he was able to comfortably get Dad into the car.

At Bill and Linda's place, Darrell wheeled Dad all around their yard for him to view it. Then Darrell and Bill lifted Dad in his wheelchair into the house and up the stairs to the main level. The joy expressed in Dad's eyes and voice from being able to see their new home was over-whelming.

After Bill got Dad back into the car, Dad said, "I think this is my last." Dad was exhausted when we got him back home and said again that he thought it was his last. When Darrell and I got him into bed that night, he was restless; he tried to get out of bed.

May 17, 2013

Dad woke at 7:00. He was very thirsty and drank a few sips of water and a little juice. He said, "I thought I left the other day." He asked me if he was in heaven. I told him no, and that he was still with us. Then he said, "I thought I was the one that was supposed to go."

I was in the kitchen when I overheard Dad ask Mom, "Do I have to go through another session like yesterday?" They were both quiet, and then Dad said, "I think I can get in the car." Mom just held his hand without saying anything. Tearfully, I added in the notebook, "He's so tired of his condition."

Later I looked into the living room and saw Dad facing Mom, lying on his side with his arm around her as she sat next to his bed in a chair. They were just silently holding each other.

Since Mom and Dad's regular pastor wasn't available, Pastor Cal Siegel came that afternoon. He approved using the song we had chosen for Dad's funeral service and then talked with Dad about cremation and letting go. It was a comforting visit that ended with a prayer while Dad held the pastor's hand.

At 7:30 that evening, Dad was finding it difficult to respond. For the first time, he tightly curled up in his bed and faced away from us. He did give Mom a kiss even though he was not talking. We called Rocky and Ricky (Dad's nephews living in Albuquerque) to let them know about Dad's decline.

Mom told us that the previous night she dreamt that I called out to her, and a little later that Shonnie did. We didn't know what to make of it. Mom said our voices were so clear to her.

May 18, 2013

Dad woke at 6:30 in the morning feeling bad because he was still in this world. He said he was "ready to go to heaven." He was wondering who had filled the hummingbird feeder; I told him Franchion had filled it yesterday.

He slept most of the day until about three o'clock when he stirred. Dad became very emotional, so torn because he felt like two people. "There must be two of me," Dad said through tears. He continued by saying, "I am standing at the foot of my bed [gestured there], and the other person is in bed. I see them both." We didn't know what he meant when Dad then asked, "How come one jar is full?"

Dad fell asleep for a while, then woke and said, "One for Marvel, one for Franchion, one for Malia..." He drifted off. When he roused again, he said, "Bill, Darrell, Aubrey... I want everyone to know I recognize them." I asked him if there was anyone with him at the foot of the bed. He squinted as if to see more clearly and replied, "Maybe a friend, maybe Arden?" *(After Dad's death, we found out Arden had died a short time later.)* Because Darrell was the newest member of the family, and before Dad fell asleep again, he said, "I want Darrell to know that he's part of the family."

Shonnie and Art arrived in the evening. Dad didn't

open his eyes but asked for a drink of water. After a couple of sips, he commented, "Nice and cold." When Shonnie and Art were getting ready to leave, Dad asked them if they were going home. He told them that he loved them, then he rolled up tightly onto his right side. Dad was unresponsive when we recited our usual prayers at his bedside, but then he said to Mom, "Good night. I love you, sweetheart." There were no words from him, only tears on his cheek when I said good night to him.

May 19, 2013

I slept every night in the living room next to Dad. At one o'clock that morning, he wanted a drink of water. I asked him about the "jar." He told me, "We're both in there." I asked him, "Who, the two of you?" He nodded yes. I was mystified. Dad thought it was seven o'clock and wondered why Mom wasn't up yet. When I told him the actual time, he asked, "How come it's so early?" Then Dad wrapped his arm around my neck and clung to me with a very long, tight hug. I'll never forget it.

Sugarfoot woke Mom that morning with her meows at Mom's bedroom door. When Dad saw Mom, he told her, "I don't understand this." A little later, he added, "I can't get started."

He talked a lot about the "two jars/bottles." It bothered him because he didn't know who was in the other one. Since we were assuming he was referring to their cremation containers, Mom and I tried to explain it was Mom in the other jar. He then seemed to remember. Dad also expressed his concerns about being cremated; Mom and I did our best to reassure him. I wasn't convinced he was settled on either issue. However, he did nod his head as if everything was okay, as he turned away from us.

Dad's nurse arrived a little later. He told her about seeing himself outside his body. She asked how he looked. Dad happily responded by saying, "Healthy."

That afternoon Dad started talking. I wrote what he told us. He "was hunting deer in the woods and in a field, pretty flowers and green, squirrels and birds, no fox, and no deer yet." He continued, "Hope I'm hunting with my '30-07' [Dad's gun was actually a 30-06], hunting alone." Then Dad looked at us and said, "I remember hunting with Keith and Clay [Franchion and Keith's son]."

May 20, 2013

Dad was always thirsty but could only drink a few sips of whatever we would bring to him. Even though he was hungry, he would shake his head "no" to the food we offered. We knew this was part of dying, but it still left us feeling helpless.

He was restless. He threw his covers back as if he wanted to get out of bed. I asked him how he felt; he said, "Frustrated." Then I asked him if he felt all mixed up. He looked at me and nodded yes. More and more, he would curl up tightly and roll onto his right side, facing the wall away from us.

Dad said, "Hi, Marvel," when she came that afternoon to stay with him while Shonnie and I took Mom shopping for clothes to wear for Dad's imminent funeral. What a bewildering experience, enjoyably shopping with Mom for an absolutely unenjoyable reason. While we were gone, Marvel said Dad asked if I had gone home.

May 21, 2013

Dad woke with soreness in his right wrist that morning from the nearly constant curling up and lying on his right side. I asked him if he would like something for the pain. He said, "I believe so." I was perplexed when he said it felt like he had a belt on. When the hospice aide came, he told her his legs didn't feel the best, that his side hurt, and that his wrist really hurt.

Diane (the social worker) arrived around noon that day. After being with Dad for a while, she knew it was going to be her last visit with him. So heartbreaking to watch her say goodbye to Dad and then to say our goodbyes to her as well.

Franchion came that evening a little after six o'clock. When Dad saw her, he said, "Hi, Frenchy." He was very weak. We gave him a few sips of water through a straw, but it was hard for him to swallow. We told him Bill had called to say hi to him; Dad simply responded by saying, "Bill." We noted that his eyes were open but "not seeing us."

At bedtime, Mom, Franchion, and I were talking to him, and he gave us kisses. He smiled, but we questioned if the smiles were for us or someone/something else. He was quite unresponsive. He started to mouth the words to our prayers but then said, "Good night, sweetheart," to Mom.

May 22, 2013

During his sleep, Dad was talking. I very clearly heard him say, "Thank you so very much." After waking, he was agonizing over the pain in his wrist. He did recognize me, Franchion, and Mom. I noted he "gave lots of kisses and good mornings" to us.

Mom put on her new outfit with the shoes Dad had given her for Mother's Day to show him. She would be wearing this for his visitation after he died. We sensed Dad realized and accepted what the new clothes were for. He was so happy she got them and delighted to see her in them! He repeatedly told her she looked beautiful and kept smiling at her. Franchion wrote, "Talked with Dad about how he would always help Mom shop and pick out something she really liked that would be different than what anyone else had." Dad kept smiling and said to Mom, "You look so pretty, sweetheart. Don't take it off." Then Darrell waltzed into the room and told Dad he got a new outfit too; Dad smiled and told him, "You have to take yours back."

While the hospice aide was caring for Dad later that morning, he told her his right wrist and elbow hurt "so bad." He asked her if someone would take his arm. Then he asked her if he was "inside out." Dad turned toward Mom and asked if he was "open here" (gesturing to his center).

*At eleven o'clock that morning, Dad desperately
called out, "Oh, help me, Lord! Oh, help me, Lord!"*

That afternoon was the last time a couple (two of Mom and Dad's close friends) came to visit. There were tears, but mostly Dad smiled a lot and was elated that they had come. Franchion noted, "Bob and Clarice here... so emotional for Dad and everyone, but was able to talk with them and tease Bob." When they were getting ready to leave, Dad told Clarice he would give her a kiss but that he wouldn't kiss Bob because he had too much goofy blood in him! As they were leaving his bedside, twice Dad called out, "God bless you!"

At 5:15, Franchion went home, so it was Mom, Darrell, and I who were with Dad while he was very peacefully sleeping; he was only taking about two shallow breaths every fifteen seconds. He looked like he was going to leave us. When Mom told him to "go ahead and go," Dad frowned, "came back" to us, and asked, "Am I open?" After our prayers with him, he faintly said, "Good night, and I love you." He fell asleep.

May 23, 2013

Dad woke me with his talking at 3:40 a.m. This is what he said, "Is this your house? Hello. Thank you." He slept again until after seven when he said, "Good morning, Malia." He looked at Darrell and said, "Good to see you." Darrell and I noticed how Dad kept smiling as he focused his attention at and across the ceiling while saying, "Yeah... Yeah..."

When Mom approached his bed, Dad smiled at her and gave her a kiss. Then he told her to "get a little closer," puckered his lips, and kissed her again!

A few minutes later, I heard him say what sounded like, "Not out today," followed with "What do you think about?" I wrote in the notebook, "His eyes are very glassy, but definitely sees something on ceiling/walls follows across the ceiling. Smiles."

About two hours later, Dad's hospice nurse arrived; Dad greeted her. She told us his BP was 92/64 and very faint to hear and that his HR was 100. Dad asked for water. The nurse told Dad she probably wouldn't see him again. To that, he responded by saying, "I'll be good."

After the nurse left, Dad's favorite aide arrived. She finished all her care duties, then asked Dad if he'd like a back rub. Dad looked at her and said, "It would feel awfully good." During the back rub, Dad kept saying, "Oh, man!" It felt so good to him. When she said goodbye to Dad, he tearfully looked at her and said, "You be a good girl." She told Dad she loved him; he said he loved her too and gave her a kiss.

Aunt Aubrey and Pastor Siegel came to visit at three o'clock. Dad was not able to respond to them. The pastor said prayers as we stood around Dad's bed.

Later, after the pastor and Aunt Aubrey had gone, Shonnie and Franchion came. Dad recognized all of us. He smiled a little as we said our prayers over him. At 10:30 p.m., he seemed to be looking at me, but I wondered if he was actually seeing someone else because Dad excitedly said, "Well, for goodness' sake, how're you doin'?"

May 24, 2013

Franchion, Darrell, and I were with Mom and Dad. Franchion and I moistened Dad's eyes with drops and swabbed his mouth. He "looked" at us, smiled, and tried to talk. He smiled again when Franchion held up Libby's funny-looking chicken toy to show him.

Dad attempted to raise his arms as if to give us hugs when we were standing around his bed. We could hear him say, "I love you." I wrote in the notebook, "He is so sweet!" Marvel arrived, and he attempted to give her a hug while we heard him say to her, "I love you."

Shonnie and Bill came that afternoon. We noticed Dad was showing mottling on the skin of his feet/heels. The hospice nurses had described mottling as red or purple blotches that would appear as Dad's death was approaching. I jotted down, "Days to live?"

It was 3:00 p.m. when Dad very clearly asked, "What day is it?" He acknowledged when I told him it was Friday the twenty-fourth of May and that it was 3:00 in the afternoon.

After everyone else left, Darrell, Mom, and I were standing around Dad's bed at 8:45. He was barely awake and barely breathing. He was staring at the upper right corner of the room when he asked, "Why am I so high?" He went on to say, "Inez doesn't know where I am." There was a brief pause, and then Dad, with his eyes open, said, "I see him ('em?)."

May 25, 2013

That morning at 6:45, I wasn't sure if Dad saw me—or someone else—what I do know is that he was talking, smiling, and laughing with others who I could not see. Dad saw Darrell and said, "Good job." As Dad looked up and to the left, this is what he said:

Doesn't make any difference... yeah, yep... love my whole family... here we go... give me a kiss... give me a kiss... (laughed and made big puckers with his lips). Oh, yeah... are you, am I... available... (animated with his hands just like in real life). I don't feel... (shook his head, saying no). Yeah (as if he doesn't feel bad or that he's okay)... (lots of "yeah, yeah")... I gotta go, you gotta go to bed... Yeah, well, I guess, kiddo.

About an hour later, I asked Dad who he had been talking to. He said he didn't know for sure. Darrell and I asked him again, and his response was, "I don't know who it is I'm talking to." Then I asked him if it was a man or a woman. Dad looked confused.

I noticed Dad was following me with his eyes when I walked around his bed. He said, "Hi, girl." I asked him if he'd like a back rub; as soon as I touched his back, he closed his eyes and smiled. I said, "Not quite as good as heaven, but..." I later jotted down Dad was certainly enjoying his new "friends," he had taken more sips of water than usual, and his eyes were relatively clear and bright that morning.

At noon Dad roused, saw Mom, and gave her a kiss. Bill came about that same time, and Aunt Aubrey came shortly after that. Since Dad appeared to be sleeping, it pleasantly surprised Bill when Dad said something that got Bill's attention. Dad turned to look at Aunt Aubrey and asked, "How're you doin'?"

We assumed Dad had fallen asleep again, so Bill was quietly chatting with Aunt Aubrey about a fawn he had seen that morning in his yard until Dad announced, "I can't hear what he's saying." Bill then gladly talked loud enough for Dad to hear!

Keith and Franchion arrived around four o'clock. Dad gave Franchion a kiss and said to Keith, "How ya doin'?" and "Oh my gosh."

When Aunt Aubrey was ready to leave, Dad gave her a kiss and told her, "You be a good girl." Those were the last words he spoke to his dear sister.

May 26, 2013

Dad slightly responded when I raised his bed that morning. His eyes were open but not focused on anything or anyone that I could identify.

Darrell drove our Lincoln (that Dad hadn't seen yet) around to the front of Mom and Dad's house, so Dad could see it out the window from his bed. Dad said, "Oh my gosh," and smiled when we talked to him about his much-loved Lincolns!

After that, Dad became more bright-eyed, smiled, and gave kisses. Mom asked him if he could see her; he responded, "Yes." Dad looked at Darrell and said, "Hi, how ya doin'?"

At noon I counted twenty seconds between two breaths. His BP was 84/56, and his HR was 108.

Keith, Franchion, Bill, and Shonnie came that day. Darrell went home. At 7:00 p.m., I noted Dad kissed me, Franchion, and Shonnie. Fifteen minutes later, when they were about to leave, Dad shook Keith's hand and kissed Shonnie, Franchion, and Bill goodbye.

It was just Mom and me, Libby and Sugarfoot in the house with Dad that night.

Monday, May 27, 2013.
"Memorial Day"

Dad was distressingly unresponsive that morning. I only noticed him grimace with pain when he was moved by the nurse and the aide. His blood pressure was 76/60, and his heart rate was 120.

Aunt Aubrey with her daughter Nance, and Nance's husband, John, stopped in. They stayed for just a short time.

When Marvel and Steve arrived, I told Dad they were there. He didn't respond. I said to him if he could hear me, to blink his eyes. He did! Marvel and Steve remained standing there for a while. As Steve remembers, "I was standing beside him, I think I may have been holding his hand. Marvel said to me, 'Tell him that you love him,' so I did. He appeared lifeless, but he surprised me and said to me, 'I love you too.' That brought tears to my eyes! I can't remember anything he may have said after that. I think of that often."

Keith needed to leave before we ate that day. This is what he shared regarding his last time with Dad:

I had a sourcing trip to Mexico scheduled and had an early Tuesday morning flight to Nogales booked. Fran-

chion and I drove to Augusta separately so I could head from Augusta to Minneapolis to catch my flight.

Dad was sleeping most of the afternoon, but when it was time for me to leave, I sat next to him to tell him I was leaving for a business trip to Mexico. He took my hand and said, "I sure wish I could go with you."

I said, "I have to leave, but I'll see you when I get back." He squeezed my hand and shook his head no. I left and spent the entire drive to Minneapolis hoping and praying that he was wrong, but I guess he knew it was not to be.

Since it was Memorial Day and we were gathered at Mom and Dad's, we decided to have an "indoor" picnic. Dad had always loved those occasions. Art charcoaled burgers and brats just outside the garage. Even with the overwhelming dread looming over us from knowing Dad was about to die, we were joking, laughing, and having an absolutely wonderful time being together. I am certain Dad was experiencing it with us!

It was four o'clock that afternoon when Franchion and I looked at Dad's legs. I noted there was "distinct mottling on both his knees."

The Rush of Wind

At 6:00 p.m., Franchion was outside (for better cell reception) talking with Keith on her phone. Mom was sitting next to Dad's bed. The rest of us were still sitting around the table. All of a sudden, I heard what I described in the notebook as "a rush of wind."

I remember leaning forward to look out the living room window by Dad's bed, truly expecting to see garbage containers tumbling on the streets engulfed in a cloud of dust, but nothing was disturbed! I looked at Steve sitting to my right and said, "What was that?" He gave me a strange look and replied, "What was what?" Then Bill exclaimed, "Yeah, what was that?" Marvel, Shonnie, Bill, and I had all heard what we said sounded like a gust of wind! Steve and Art hadn't heard anything.

Franchion was wondering what we were so excitedly talking about when she came back into the house. Those of us who had experienced it told her that a gust of wind came from the kitchen, went through the dining area, and into the living room where Dad and Mom were! I don't *know* what that "wind" was. I *believe* it was angels arriving to prepare Dad for the transition from this life to his new life.

Interestingly, it was just the previous day from writing this section about the "wind" that I was looking through some of the books Darrell and I have. I was measuring them, looking at the word and page counts, etc., when I noticed a bookmark. It had been placed in the pages of one of the books that I don't remember ever starting to read; it was one of Darrell's books. The bookmark was a Bible verse regarding "wind" I had laminated onto a small piece of paper shortly after Dad died. I had forgotten about it. Amazingly it resurfaced at that exact time! This is a photo of the bookmark:

"Then a wind lifted me up, and I heard behind me a fierce rushing sound as the glory of the Lord rose from his place. I heard the sound of the living creatures' wings brushing against one another, the sound of the wheels beside them, and a fierce rushing sound. A wind lifted me and carried me along, and I went full of exaltation, the hand of the Lord strong upon me" (Ezekiel 3:12-14).

Franchion and I stayed with Mom and Dad that night. Dad was completely unresponsive. Mom retired to the bedroom, and Franchion and I remained in the living room.

Dad's Final Moments

Dad's breathing had changed from deep rhythmic noises to shallow, irregularly spaced sounds. Franchion and I immediately jumped up and looked at Dad. We noted the time; it was 2:30 a.m. Franchion got Mom up. As the three of us stood around Dad's bed, we watched his breathing continue to get weaker and weaker. He was very peaceful. There were no gasps or struggles of any kind. Eventually, he was only taking almost silent little puffs of air. He resembled a baby bird anticipating nourishment from a parent.

We were talking to him. We were touching him. Franchion held up his hand to me so I could see that his fingernails were purple. At 2:50 a.m., Dad's puffs ceased. He was finally, beautifully ushered away by the angels. The same angels I believe we were blessed to have heard when they arrived the previous evening.

Mom held Sugarfoot up to peer into Dad's face. Mom told her he was gone. "Suggi" looked at him for a few seconds, then turned to face Mom. So sweetly, Sugarfoot reached up with her paw and touched Mom's cheek.

May 28, 2013

We called Marvel, Shonnie, and Bill to let them know Dad had died. Shonnie, Bill, and Marvel with Steve all arrived by 3:45 that morning. We quietly visited, comforted by the presence of Dad's body still with us.

Birds outside started singing at 4:26 a.m. as if to remind us we had things we needed to take care of. One of us called hospice to let them know Dad was gone. The nurse arrived at 6:20 to officially verify that Dad had died. Maureen, of Anderson Funeral Home, was called; she arrived at 7:15.

Maureen kindly asked if we'd like to go into a bedroom while she removed Dad's body from the house. We all said we'd prefer to stay in the room with Dad. Shonnie helped Maureen lift Dad's body from his bed onto the funeral home gurney. Our faces were in the window as we watched Maureen place Dad into the van and drive the one block to the funeral home and back into the home's underground garage to take care of Dad's body.

At 9:30 a.m., Franchion jotted in the notebook that a little male hummingbird had come to the feeder; we hadn't seen one for days. She also wrote that the previous day there "were so many blossoms on the hibiscus. Today there are none."

Maureen came back at 2:30 p.m. to finalize funeral plans for Dad. It didn't take very long since Mom and Dad had already taken care of most of those choices with her some time ago.

However, Maureen did suggest using one larger cremation vault for both Dad's and (then later) Mom's remains, rather than two small separate vaults. We wondered if Dad could have been referring to that when he'd talked about the two jars/containers and saying, "We're both in there."

Mom, Marvel, Franchion, Shonnie, and I walked the two blocks from Mom's and (still, it seemed) Dad's house to the local floral shop. We ordered flowers for Dad's funeral. It was a pleasant, intimate time for us.

Before Shonnie left that day, she remembered Mom feeling bad; Mom told Shonnie, "I hardly talked to Dad all day the day before he died." So sad for Mom. She loved Dad so very, very much. And Dad absolutely knew that.

When Franchion and Keith's two sons, Nick and Clay, arrived at about six o'clock, they walked with Franchion, Mom, Darrell, and me to the funeral home to see Dad. It was the last time Nick and Clay saw their grandpa.

May 29, 2013

Hospice had made arrangements to have Dad's hospital bed and wheelchair ramp picked up at 10:00 a.m. It was a very simple and easy physical thing to watch that, at the same time, elicited a heart-rending emotional response.

Darrell vacuumed the carpeting, then helped Mom rearrange the furniture to fill the empty space where Dad's bed had been for months. Mom and I cleared all Dad's medical supplies, etc., from the living room and from the kitchen breakfast bar. It was extremely painful to ignore the voice inside me screaming, "Wait... Dad needs this stuff!"

Aunt Aubrey came in the afternoon. Darrell and I, Mom, and Aunt Aubrey walked to the funeral home to be with Dad's body. Darrell and I went back to the house while Mom and Aunt Aubrey went to the floral shop. Aunt Aubrey wanted to get flowers for Dad. Since she and Mom had always had a wonderful relationship, it was good for them to have some time alone.

May 30, 2013

Marvel and Steve, with their son, Casey, and their daughter, Mindi, along with her husband, Bill, and their two sons, Owen and Caleb, arrived at Mom's house that morning. At 10:30, Mom, Darrell, and I walked with them one last time to be with Dad. That afternoon Maureen took Dad's body to be cremated in Eau Claire.

May 31, 2013

Shortly after noon, Darrell and I, Art, and Casey went to the church to set up the screen and projector to have it ready to play the video for Dad's funeral service.

Bill and Linda parked their car at Mom and Dad's house and walked with Mom, Darrell, and me to the funeral home at 3:35 for Dad's visitation. The rest of the family met us there.

Maureen and Trenton had created a stunning gathering room for us to enter! The overwhelming number of flowers and plants, the lights, the photos were all so exquisitely arranged, with Dad's cremation box front and center. An endless line of friends and family members came during the visitation between four and eight o'clock.

During the visitation, there was an intense thunderstorm with small hail and a heavy downpour of rain. By the time we left the funeral home, the storm was over. The sun had come out. It was illuminating a brilliant double rainbow and lingering super-puffed mammatus clouds!

Saturday, June 1, 2013

It was 9:20 a.m. when Darrell drove me, Bill and Linda, and Mom the short distance across town to Grace Lutheran Church in Augusta, Wisconsin, for Dad's funeral. More than 200 people attended the visitation and/or the funeral. The service was impeccable and harrowing. Dad was there, and Dad wasn't with us.

We recalled the dream Dad told us about on May 15, "There was a funeral, and all of us kids were there and two pastors." And on May 17, I wrote, "Since Mom and Dad's regular pastor wasn't available, Pastor Cal Siegel came that afternoon." It was also Pastor Siegel who officiated the funeral and not their regular pastor.

The service concluded graveside at Thompson Valley Cemetery, located about five miles out of town between Augusta and Osseo. As we walked into the cemetery, our attention was drawn ahead and upward where Joe Haak (the father to some of Mom and Dad's great-grandchildren) stood in traditional dress, playing a beautiful Christian tune on his bagpipe. Only the funeral director had known he was going to do that. What an incredibly magnificent honor for Dad! What a tremendously memorable sight and sound for us!

The notebook entries for Dad ended

Part 2: Mom

Mom's About to Die

I was not aware of the weather outside even though it was -4°F, windy, and snowing in Augusta, Wisconsin, on February 19, 2015.

The hospice nurse arrived in the afternoon to check Mom. She showed me the mottling that had begun on Mom's legs and told me she thought Mom would go that night. After the nurse left, I sat next to Mom's bed, talking to her. She moved her hand and made a sound as if to say something; she appeared to be teary/emotional.

I noted at 2:15, Mom's breathing changed; it sounded "like a little propeller running all the time in the back of her throat."

I continued talking to Mom about memories and heaven. Her lips moved without making a sound. At 3:15 p.m., I saw large purple patches on both of her feet. I gave her some morphine just in case she might be uncomfortable and called my siblings.

Five: November 2014

Seven Months Earlier

Mom, 90 years old, so vibrant and healthy-looking, point-

ing to Dad's name on hospice quilt

April 2014

Dr. Halverson

Franchion remembered that at one of the last appointments with Dr. Halverson (it may have been the last one), Mom was already considered terminal and asked Dr. Halverson how much longer he thought she had. He responded, "Maybe a year."

When Mom repeated that back to him, he took her hands and shook his head yes. She looked directly into his eyes, then teared up, but accepted that without any more questions. He said he was sorry and that he was glad to have met both Dad and Mom and to have had them as his patients. I had tears rolling down my cheeks too. It was a very special moment between them. Dr. Halverson was such a great and caring man.

Mom's Stroke

Mom, like Dad, was referred to St. Joseph Hospice out of Chippewa Falls, Wisconsin. Franchion drove to Mom's house on November 11 to set her up with their care. It was comforting to be with people who were already incredibly dear to us, having guided us through Dad's journey. Mom was doing well living alone since Dad died, so she told Franchion to go ahead and go home at one o'clock that afternoon.

Sometime between Franchion's departure and Marvel's arrival the following morning, Mom fell. Marvel said the drapes in the house were closed, and the television was on. Mom's walker was tipped over by a large plant near the front door, and the end table by the loveseat was out of place. Mom was sitting on the floor with her back leaning onto the front of the loveseat, with sweet Sugarfoot lying on the loveseat directly above Mom.

Marvel called 911, and Mom was taken to the hospital in Eau Claire. She most likely had suffered a stroke, or possibly cancer had metastasized to her brain/spine. Her speech was slurred, and her right side was very weak.

It was remarkable that Mom had been set up with hospice care just the day before. Nobody knew we'd be needing their assistance so soon.

Shonnie and Marvel stayed at the hospital with Mom during visiting hours for the two days she was their patient. Darrell and I took her home after she was discharged on November 14.

Mom was doing well. Bill and Marvel were at her house when we arrived there that afternoon. Then Marvel's daughter, Jenni, with her two daughters, Emma and Leah, came to see Mom. Shonnie and Art also visited. Mom loved seeing everyone!

The next morning, Mom signed her do-not-resuscitate order (DNR). Bill and Linda came. Mom did great that day, taking care of herself and eating well. But by that evening, she was struggling with her speech, her eyesight, her walking; and she was more confused.

November 16–18, 2019

It was not difficult setting up our care routine for Mom. We used what we had learned from our experience with Dad. The notebook was again placed on the breakfast counter and opened to a new page, following where the entries for Dad had ended to where the entries for Mom had already begun.

The hospice caregivers told us to have Mom read to us and practice tongue twisters and rhymes to help her speech. They also showed us eye, finger, and arm exercises and stretches to improve Mom's affected right side.

Mom was doing fine again the morning of November 16. I went home after Shonnie arrived. Shonnie jotted down that "Marvel, Jenni, and the girls here watching Packer game. Good day! Ate well." Later that day, Shonnie recalled:

There were always a couple of daily devotional booklets in the house. She liked it when I'd read it to her, but I wanted her to read to me. You know she didn't enjoy it, but she did alright.

I'm not sure what scripture we were reading. Afterward, I said, "Just think of all the people you're going to meet in heaven. Jesus and all His disciples." Her eyes got big and bright, and she said, "Do you think I'm going to meet *them?" I said, "I think you will." It was a happy moment knowing she had the realization of the endless possibilities that awaited.*

Franchion came to stay with Mom on November 17. She wrote that Mom was up and walked, with the assistance of her walker, around the living room and that she chatted with friends who phoned in the afternoon.

Franchion noted Mom was very tired after reading from a children's book and a prayer book and after practicing tongue twisters on both November 17 and 18.

November 19–26, 2014

During a restless night, Franchion heard Mom yell out a friend's name several times. However, when Mom woke up, she told Franchion she'd had a dream about Marvel.

The following morning, Franchion saw that Mom was completely soaked through her adult diapers, the robe she'd slept in, and her bedsheets. Franchion wrote, "Going to try to figure out Mom's washing machine for sheets and robe." It had also snowed, so Steve came and shoveled Mom's driveway and sidewalk.

Since cold and flu season had begun, the hospice nurse reminded Marvel to tell us, "Anyone sick, don't come!" Thankfully, none of us became infected.

This is how Bill announced his arrival on Friday, November 21:

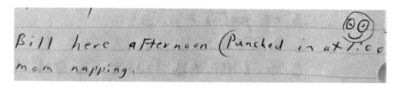

Like the rest of us, Bill worked with Mom on her walking, speech, and fingers/arm exercises and stretches. Shonnie also brought her computer for Mom to play games on. But Mom's favorite exercise was petting or combing Sugarfoot.

Thanksgiving, 2014

Thanksgiving Day was the twenty-seventh of November in 2014. Darrel and I, with our "foster-failure" dog, Lambeau, arrived at Mom's house at 11:15. Since it was a holiday, Meals on Wheels didn't make a delivery. Darrell went to the convenience store in town and bought us frozen turkey dinners. Mom said hers tasted good! During the afternoon, she put Christmas puzzles together on the computer. It was a nice, quiet day.

The following Saturday, November 29, we got together at Mom's house for our Thanksgiving dinner at noon. This is who came: Marvel and Steve, Kevin and Paula with Lexie, Mitch and Paula with Riley and Avery, Franchion and Keith, Shonnie and Art, Peter and Jessie, Bill and Linda, and Darrell and I. Mom enjoyed her meal and seeing everyone, but she tired quickly and slept from 1:45–4:30 that afternoon.

Mom did well talking on the phone, which was wonderful. So many friends and extended family members called and/or visited to wish her a happy Thanksgiving.

Six: December 2019

Mom and Sugarfoot

Word Finding

Mom was progressively having more difficulty finding the right words for what she was trying to say. She knew the correct words in her mind, but that wasn't always what she voiced. Fortunately, she would laugh or giggle at herself when she knew something hadn't come out correctly.

Mom began to say "White Hook" instead of "Sugarfoot" when referring to her kitty. Franchion explained that before Mom's stroke, she "would ask me to help her clip Sugarfoot's 'fish hooks' (that's what Mom called them) when they started to get too long and started to catch on everything. It was a challenge because they were so white in her white paws. Mom would hold her, and I would do my best to find them to clip. It was cute how she became 'White Hook' after her stroke."

Mom and I got to laughing so hard one afternoon. She repeatedly asked, "Do I have to do those *dishes?*" Every time I would respond by saying no. *Finally,* I realized Mom was trying to ask if she had to do those (finger/hand) *stretches.*

"Whistling" was the word Mom used for dreaming. She called prune juice "vanilla" and the nursing home "the park." "Bunting" is what Mom would often substitute for any word she couldn't vocalize. Bunting became her go-to word due to repeating it for many of the words that had the letter "B" in a nursery rhyme we'd have her read to us. She got to giggling one time when she said, "I'll have a 'bunting' for dinner." She was trying to say "donut."

Mom worked hard trying to improve her communication difficulties by practicing reading and saying tongue twisters.

Challenging

There were some challenging times caring for Mom which became endearing and amusing as we thought back.

She was watching me as I was doing the dishes in the kitchen. She got a little upset because she thought I was taking too long to finish the job.

Bill mentioned a time he was staying overnight with Mom, and "no matter what I did, I couldn't get her blanket right. I know she was frustrated, and so was I." Bill added, "I always felt bad about it."

Franchion shared how she would pour a cup of coffee for Mom and then need to reheat it about four times before Mom would finish it!

Shonnie followed by declaring, "And Mom wanted that second cup of hot coffee *just* as you were going to sit down." Shonnie also recalled Mom would get a little impatient if her Meals on Wheels were not delivered exactly on time.

December 1-23, 2019

The nurse thought Mom had a mini-stroke, or possibly cancer had affected a blood vessel in her brain around December 12. Her ability to talk was noticeably worse; she was unable to say our names at times. We also noticed that her right hand would sometimes slip off the walker as she stood; Mom wasn't aware of that happening.

On December 13, Mom and I read together numerous Christmas cards she had received. They were beautiful cards with heartfelt messages and personal handwritten blessings added. It was extremely emotional reviewing them. We cried.

That afternoon it was heart-wrenching listening to a phone conversation Mom had with one of her closest friends. They had both lost their husbands, and now Mom was dying. They were struggling with how much their lives had changed but so thankful for the cherished memories they could still share with each other.

Marvel was with Mom on December 17 when Linda (Mom's niece) called. Linda had recently found out about Mom's stroke. She wanted Mom to know that her dad, Alvin (Mom's brother), would be in Augusta for Christmas and that he planned to see Mom during that time. At 11:45 that night, Marvel heard Mom call out Alvin's name twice.

A few days later, on December 21, *Mom first mentioned her sister, Virginia.* Shonnie was staying at Mom's and, at 8:30 a.m., noted, "[Mom] says she was half-dreaming that Virginia [Aunt Ginny] was here." We don't remember Mom ever referring to her sister as Virginia, only as Ginny. Virginia/Ginny had died on February 18, 2010.

Keith drove Franchion and their dog, Lucy, to Mom's house on December 22. Franchion wrote, "Told Mom Keith and Lucy brought me today (Lucy rode along. Mom thought I said, 'Keith mowed the lawn')."

That afternoon, Mom asked Franchion to pluck a couple of hairs off her face. Because Franchion's hands were a bit shaky, she was having trouble zeroing in on them and was concerned about pinching Mom's skin. Mom lovingly suggested they try it again later.

Kay, Virginia's daughter (Mom's niece), came to stay with Mom for a couple of hours. Keith and Franchion needed to leave at 3:00, and Marvel couldn't get there until 5:00. It was a nice time for Mom and Kay to visit.

Christmas 2019

Pastor Wessel arrived at 11:30 a.m. on December 24 to give Mom communion and to pray with her. Marvel, Shonnie, and Art were also there. Marvel went home before Darrell and I arrived at 12:30. Art needed to leave since he was part of the church service in Eau Claire, where he and Shonnie attended.

As recorded in the notebook, by four o'clock on Christmas Eve, Marvel and Steve, Kevin and Paula with Lexi, Mitch and Paula with Riley and Avery, Casey, Franchion and Keith, Darrell and I, Shonnie, and Bill and Linda were together with Mom.

At seven o'clock, we lit a candle for Mom to hold. All the lights in the house were turned off. After lining up one by one, we each lit our candle from hers. We sang a heavenly Christmas hymn together (twice) while Darrell accompanied on his guitar. It was beautiful. It was significant.

Bill and Mom (front), Malia, Marvel, Franchion,

Shonnie (back, left to right) December 24, 2014

Sugarfoot woke Mom on Christmas morning by jump-
ing up on her bed. At 10:00, Mom was so happy to see her
brother, Alvin, when he stopped in! He stayed for just an
hour. It was immensely painful for both Uncle Alvin and
Mom when they said goodbye to each other.

Darrell and I played a game Mom and Dad had loved
to play with Mom during the afternoon. Later, when it was
dark outside, we took Mom to Chippewa Falls to drive

through Irvine Park. Entering the park, and continuing the tour through it, transported us into a Christmas fantasy world of dazzling lights, beautiful music, and festive decorations! Mom was her old self during those few hours; she was energetic and appeared to be healthy!

End of December 2019

On December 27, Darrell and I took Mom to Marvel and Steve's house. It was a beautiful morning with fresh snow blanketing everything. Marvel and Steve's kids, Kevin, Jenni, Mitch, Mindi, and Casey along with *their* kids were there to spend time with Mom. We stayed from noon until 3:30. Mom was napping at home by 4:00. After Mom went to bed that evening, I noted Mom was "quite mixed up talking tonight. Seemed a bit flushed in her face and breathing harder."

Shonnie arrived to stay with Mom the following morning. She wrote that Art and Peter (Shonnie and Art's son) came for a short visit.

Keith dropped Franchion off the morning of December 29. Diane (the social worker) arrived and said she thought Mom would have a gradual decline, just like Dad. She also noticed that Mom's talking seemed more difficult.

Mom continued doing what she could to improve her condition. I think she was still processing the fact that she was actually going to die. Franchion wrote Mom did six laps around the house with her walker after Diane left and before the nurse came.

Mom admitted to the nurse she was aware of her worsening speech and breathing capability. The nurse reiterated to Franchion and Mom that Mom's symptoms are classic for stroke, but they could also be due to a brain tumor pressing against a blood vessel.

That night before going to sleep, Mom told Franchion she "is hoping to talk better tomorrow." Franchion added, "Me too!"

New Year's Eve 2019

On New Year's Eve morning, Mom announced that she had "really slept" the previous night, but she'd had a lot of dreams. Franchion wrote what Mom said, "Rodell, in the house when they were kids with Grandpa and Grandma." Rodell was a train stop between Eau Claire and Augusta, where Mom grew up, and she was referring to her parents when she said, "Grandpa and Grandma." Franchion added Mom couldn't tell her what they were doing in the dream. She was only able to say a few words without finishing any sentences.

A short time later, when Mom was ready to take a nap, she asked Franchion about her always turning to face the window to sleep. Franchion told her that was the way Dad slept. Mom remembered.

After Mom woke from her nap, Franchion noted Mom's left eye seemed to be more open than her right eye. She remarked to Franchion, "It felt different."

Shonnie checked in to stay with Mom for the rest of that day and for overnight. She overheard a phone conversation Mom had with a friend during the afternoon; she was a close friend of Mom's since they had been in high school together and whose husband had also died. They were reminiscing about all the New Year's Eve nights they had spent laughing and playing cards together.

Seven: January 2015

New Year's Day 2015

Before Shonnie left, she and Mom watched the New Year's Day parade on TV, something we had always done when we were kids. Mom got teary-eyed.

Marvel was caring for Mom that afternoon when Mom said she "felt funny." She could only do one lap with her walker around the house before returning to her chair. She became very emotional. She cried. Marvel wrote that Mom was "very confused about almost everything."

Mom was upset because the "TV people" kept talking about 2015. She was convinced they were wrong because, to her, it was 2004.

Marvel also wrote that Mom was worried about her hearing aids: "She did not want them to stop working."

January 2–15, 2015

Bill arrived at 11:15 a.m. to take over for Marvel on January 2. He recalled Mom telling him, "Your hands look just like Dad's." It was an endearing comment for Bill. He stayed with Mom until Shonnie came the next afternoon.

Remembering Dad's awful problem with his bowels, we did our best to monitor Mom's. Shonnie was reviewing the notebook when she noticed an interesting entry Bill had made:

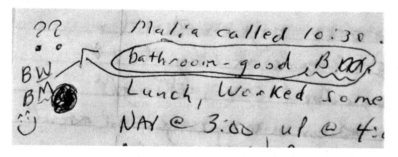

On Monday, the fifth of January, Franchion called Mayo Clinic in Eau Claire to talk with someone regarding Mom's pacemaker check that was scheduled for January 14. Franchion had jotted down on the reminder letter, "Top two chambers of the heart, working on their own. The pacemaker keeps bottom two chambers working."

The doctor reassured her that since Mom never had problems with her device, he felt a check was not necessary and that the battery should function okay for as long as she would need it. Mom's January 14 appointment was canceled.

Mom was having trouble saying our names again and with speaking in general on January 7. Franchion wrote, "Trying to tell me something, couldn't get complete thought out or sentence out, got teary-eyed, said she wished she could talk like before. Knows it is easier to talk with someone over the phone or if someone stops in to visit with her."

That afternoon Marvel was with Mom when Mom said, "The star on the tree was new." The star hadn't been changed. Marvel also noted that Mom couldn't see the light changes on the tree until she removed her glasses.

Mom did relatively well walking with her walker around the house and doing her exercises, etc. It was her speaking that remained the most difficult and frustrating for her. She was unable to tell me something on January 9; I handed her a piece of paper and a pen and told her to try writing it down. She did! She wrote, "Get meal." She was hungry! Sadly, her right hand became too weak to continue writing legibly.

It was troubling to realize Mom's vision changes were upsetting her more than we knew. Shonnie wrote on January 11, "Mom is talking about double vision, but not all the time. She says she's had it about two weeks!"

Exactly at midnight on the night of January 14, Marvel heard the radio Mom and Dad always kept in their bedroom begin to play. She went into the room and turned it off. Marvel noted, "Sugarfoot? Nothing seemed out of place!" The very next night, January 15, when Shonnie was staying with Mom, the radio began to play again exactly at midnight. Mom was sleeping in the living room during this time. Shonnie remarked, "Sugarfoot wasn't there, two nights in a row?" *That had never happened before, and it never happened again.*

January 16–25, 2015

Mom tried to explain more about her vision problems to Bill on January 16. Bill jotted in the notebook, "Says she has trouble with her vision when not looking straight on but at an angle."

We didn't know if Mom could read to herself. She never complained about *not* being able to read to herself. Franchion wrote on January 20 that Mom was in her recliner looking at a local advertising paper. Later that day, Franchion noted Mom called two friends to thank them for the lovely flowers they had brought for her a couple of days earlier. Mom certainly appreciated her many thoughtful and caring friends.

When we were very young, we had a sweet dog named Joker. Franchion would bring their dog, Lucy, with her when she was caring for Mom. Franchion wrote on January 21 that Mom was calling Lucy "Joker."

It was on January 22 when Mom said she couldn't "hear" me, that she didn't like the sound of my voice. She said she could hear Darrell. I wondered if it was due to the tone of my voice and her hearing aid settings. Disheartening.

Bedroom

We had automatically set up Mom's hospital bed in the living room where Dad's had been. She didn't seem to mind until the TV light or other lights in the kitchen/dining area began to disturb her nighttime sleep.

It would be dark outside before 5:00, and Mom would usually go to bed a couple of hours later. That's when the TV became a source of entertainment for us.

Marvel and Steve came over one evening when Darrell and I were there. After Mom went to bed, we started to play a game Marvel and Steve had brought with them. We had so much fun, but Mom said the light bothered her.

Since Mom would sit in her recliner or rocking chair during the daytime, we moved her hospital bed into the bedroom on January 23. A bell was placed within her reach to ring if she needed anything. She could sleep without us disturbing her, and we could enjoy evening entertainment.

Our Names

After breakfast on January 24, Mom could not think of my name. Eventually, she said, "Marvel and Steve." I asked her if she knew her son's name; she said "Bill," followed with "Bill and Linda," then "Franchion and Keith." She could not think of Shonnie's name either.

Mom thought for a while, and then she very slowly started to sound out, "Ma... r... vel." Her eyes brightened. She looked at me, smiled, and said, "Malia." Mom was so happy to be able to clearly say, "Malia and Darrell... Shonnie and Art!" The effort it took exhausted her; she took a nap and slept until noon.

Mom's Ninety-First Birthday

January 24 was also the day we chose to celebrate Mom's ninety-first birthday. I don't remember if we chose a week early due to our schedules or if we were concerned Mom's health could rapidly decline. Anyway, we celebrated her birthday that evening rather than on her actual birthday, January 31.

Mom was all dressed and ready to leave for a supper club near Fall Creek by 1:40 that afternoon, even though we weren't leaving until 4:10; she was excited about the outing! She wanted to stay awake until we left, but by 2:15, she was napping.

Marvel and Steve, Franchion and Keith, Darrell and I, Shonnie and Art, and Bill and Linda gathered at the supper club for a wonderful celebration of Mom's ninety-one years of life! Even though Mom felt embarrassed because she needed assistance with her walking and ordering her food, she enjoyed the party. She ended the dinner with her favorite treat, a Pink Squirrel with an added birthday candle!

January 26-31, 2015

Franchion was caring for Mom during Diane's visit on January 26. Mom was reassured that she would *not* be taken off hospice care (something that was troubling her).

Mom was also told not to worry about losing weight, that it was normal, just like it had been for Dad. Diane comforted Mom by telling her to simply "eat what she wanted when she wanted."

Franchion asked Diane what hospice service was available for Mom if none of us were able to care for her at some time. Franchion was told that St. Joseph Hospice could offer a room for up to five days once every ninety days.

That afternoon Franchion explained the service to Mom. She was very receptive to it and thought it was a very nice part of hospice care. Mom said it would be fine with her. I think Mom thought of it as a mini-vacation (she died before we ever used the service).

For the next couple of days, Mom was more emotional. Franchion noted, "Mom was wondering how things are going to be." And after Franchion finished putting the laundry away one day, she wrote that Mom "wished she could do it and other things like before. Said she guessed she cries because of us kids, Sugarfoot, and not knowing how long this will go on." Franchion assured her Sugarfoot would have a loving home with her and Keith; that gave her a great sense of relief. We all did our best to comfort Mom by listening to her, by touching and hugging her, by expressing our love for her, and by crying with her.

On January 30, Shonnie wrote that the nurse talked with Mom "about how things might not improve and how she has to adjust to how she is now." Shonnie continued, "Also, how all of us have to adjust (one of the hardest things we'll ever have to do)."

Mom received many cards and phone calls from friends and from Aunt Aubrey for her birthday. One friend delivered a birthday cake. She was overjoyed when another friend sang a special birthday song to her over the phone. Kay stopped in to give her a card with a box of candy. Meals on Wheels added a birthday cupcake and card to Mom's meal. And Uncle Alvin surprised her with a visit; she was elated to see him!

Eight: February 2015

A Good Day

Diane arrived to talk with Mom on the second day of February. Franchion was there and noted that it was a good visit, even though it was with lots of tears. Kay stopped in again for a short time. That afternoon Mom and Franchion discussed the comparisons between how things were going for Mom with how things had gone for Dad.

During the evening, Mom was able to speak relatively well. She and Franchion talked about the chats with Diane and Kay earlier and about Uncle Alvin's surprise visit for her birthday. Mom said she would enjoy going out again with all of us like we'd done to celebrate her birthday. Franchion then added that Mom "wanted to look in [her] closet at her clothes."

The next morning Mom picked out a blouse and a nice pair of slacks to wear. She told Franchion she felt good about being "dressed." Mom had a good day until that evening.

Gibberish

It was approximately 5:30 that evening when Mom told Franchion she wanted to do some laps with her walker around the house. Franchion described what happened:

Mom was walking slower than usual and not picking her feet up much. I had my hands on her waist. She kind of stumbled forward. I helped catch her. I asked her if she felt more tired tonight. She didn't know. Mom wasn't able to speak clearly. She teared up and kept trying to talk... kept getting worse... sounded more like gibberish. I could barely make out any words. She could understand me. I kept reassuring her that everything would be okay. We all have to take it just one day at a time and be thankful for this time, to try and not worry about the way things are going to be because none of us know.

She was trying to say so much, going on and on. [I] got her ready for bed. [She] started to cry. She looked directly into my eyes, trying so hard to talk. All I could do was hug her and tell her how much we all love her and that things would be better in the morning after a good night's sleep, and we would talk then.

Franchion added that Mom did acknowledge everything she was saying and that she smiled when Franchion went to the door to leave before turning out the light.

Virginia!

Franchion returned to Mom's bedroom at 10:15 because she thought Mom was dreaming and calling out "Virginia!" in her sleep. However, when Franchion got to the bedroom door, she found Mom sitting on the edge of her bed as she did when she was ready to get up for the day. Franchion wrote that Mom kept repeating "Virginia!" over and over and that she had a "kind of different look in her eyes." Franchion stayed in Mom's bedroom and turned on one of the lights in the attached bathroom to serve as a night light. By 10:30, Mom was back to sleep.

It was almost midnight when she stirred again. Franchion noted how Mom reached out for her hands—with an unusually soft and caressingly gentle touch—and tried to pull herself up. After reassuring Mom that everything was fine and telling her that she was sleeping on the floor near her, Mom fell back to sleep.

One more time that night, about half an hour later, Mom tried to sit up. Franchion showed her the time and said they needed to go back to sleep. Mom finally slept soundly the rest of the night. *Mom was not taking any morphine or other pain medications during this time.*

February 4, 2015

The next morning, February 4, Franchion wrote Mom was able to respond by saying, "Yes, no, okay," and "Virginia." Franchion asked Mom if she'd had any dreams the previous night. Mom responded by saying she "wasn't sure."

However, when Franchion asked her if she had seen Virginia, Mom's eyes lit up, and she exclaimed, "Yes!" Franchion wrote:

[She] kept repeating "Virginia!" and reaching her hand out. I asked her if she had touched her, and she said yes. I asked her if she had seen anyone else (Grandpa and Grandma or Dad), said no. I clarified again if she had seen and talked with and touched Virginia, her sister, and she said yes.

Franchion then noted:

Maybe when she took my hand last night, it was as if she was touching her [Virginia]. [She] wanted to talk more, but [Mom could only respond with] "I could" or "I would" or "I wish" was all I could make out.

Eleven-thirty that morning, the nurse arrived. She told Franchion, after speaking with her supervisor, they felt Mom had suffered another mini-stroke the previous evening. The nurse went on by explaining it can become a pattern after an initial stroke. Mom's initial stroke was November 11, 2014, followed by a mini-stroke on December 13, 2014, and another one on February 3, 2015.

During the afternoon, when Franchion was making tea, she noticed Mom was relaxing in her recliner, petting Sugarfoot on her lap. Franchion overheard Mom chuckle and clearly said, "I like you... I like you" to her sweet kitty.

After they had tea, Mom tried to say something about Virginia again. Franchion asked Mom if Virginia looked good. Mom responded, "She sure did!" Mom said, "Virginia and Kay." Franchion told Mom that the next time Kay came, she would be happy to know that Mom had seen *her* mom. She nodded yes.

At bedtime, Franchion wrote Mom "was able to say some of [the] prayer tonight. Then, from out of nowhere, she said, 'I thought I would get a cold, but I didn't.' Few tears. Asleep."

February 5-8, 2015

On February 5, after eating breakfast, Mom told Franchion she slept "very good" during the night. Franchion asked her if Virginia had come again. Mom replied, "No, and isn't that something."

Franchion noted, "This morning [Mom] doesn't think she saw or talked with her, just that she was so on her mind, but that it was good. Not sure she wants to talk about Virginia today." Franchion jotted in the margin of the notebook. Mom commented, "So real, but hard to believe." Perhaps Mom was worried we might think she could be "losing her mind." She had voiced that concern about Dad when he described extraordinary things.

However, that evening after supper, Marvel was with Mom when she talked about Virginia again. Marvel wrote what Mom added about the visit: "She was about fifty years old and sat on [the] loveseat with Mom. She had a purse with her." Shonnie's comment after reading that, "Wow, Aunt Ginny travels pretty light!"

Bill was staying with Mom on February 6 when Aunt Aubrey stopped in. He wrote, "Aubrey, Mom, and I talked a lot and laughed." Mom enjoyed the visit; it was so good for Mom.

Marvel came to stay with Mom on February 7. Marvel

noted, "Mom wants to talk. She's doing it much better but coughing about every half hour after going to bed."

After church on February 8, Kay brought the church directory to go over pictures in it with Mom. Mom enjoyed it. How thoughtful of Kay!

Diane's Visit

On February 9, Franchion was caring for Mom when Diane came. This is how Franchion summarized the meeting:

"Happy" visit with Diane. Mom brought up Virginia, we talked more about it, and Diane reassured Mom this was normal for people to experience at this time in their lives.

Mom was wondering why she didn't see someone she was closer to—she and Virginia were not that close—even though they were sisters. Diane said she may have been the first one to come to her to let her know everything would be okay and she would be there when the time came for Mom. I said she was an older sister and was the more "bossy" one in the family, especially to Mom. Diane said that would make sense.

Mom understood and knows this is not unusual—but doesn't remember visits Dad talked about—Diane told her it was not surprising she did not remember things Dad had experienced because she was trying to process and handle so much that was happening with Dad.

Mom asked if the time was getting closer to leaving this world. Diane said she felt it would be "months," not days or weeks, and that she would let her know when the time was getting closer and for her not to worry. Mom agreed.

Mom did not remember crying and feeling sad or emotional last week just knows she feels good now. Diane also told Mom she might have visits from others and that this does not necessarily mean that her time is going to end soon and that she should take comfort in them.

A few hours after Diane left, Mom started talking with Franchion about Rodell, where she grew up, and about when she was a kid with her siblings. She talked about her grandparents and her aunts and uncles—clearly recalling all their names, ages, and interesting things about them. Franchion was amazed by how clear Mom's memory was and how easily she could communicate that day!

February 10-11, 2015

Mom was more tired the next day, February 10. At midnight, Franchion heard Mom's bell ring. Mom told her that her stomach hurt. After Franchion helped Mom to the bathroom, then back to her bed, she slept until 6:15.

That's when Franchion found Mom sitting on the toilet in the bathroom of the bedroom. She had not rung her bell or called out for help. Franchion surmised Mom was testing her strength; she needed to evaluate her physical abilities. After Franchion got Mom back into bed, she wrote, "[Mom] said she thought she was stronger than that... now she knows she is not. Took a lot out of her, said she would not do that again." I believe, after having tested herself, Mom now accepted that she was not going to get better and that she truly was dying.

At 8:45, Mom was "up" and not feeling well at all. Franchion noted that she was "very weak and wasn't sure she could even stand up. She sat on the side of the bed, felt like throwing up... Says middle of chest hurts."

A little later, after Franchion got her into her recliner, she added that Mom was "just kind of moaning with eyes closed and hands across her chest."

Franchion called the nurse. A low dose of morphine was ordered so that, according to the nurse, even if Mom didn't need it now, she'd have it for later. The nurse informed Franchion it could be a "bug" or it could be cancer. Franchion noticed that even though Mom fell asleep, she would open her eyes; they were "glassy."

Since she was too weak to walk, a commode was brought into the living room and placed near Mom's recliner for her to use.

It was 11:15 when Mom said her chest didn't hurt as much, but by 11:30, Franchion wrote she was "holding her head with her hand. I asked if her head hurt, she said, 'Yes, I guess it does.'" About an hour later, when Mom roused, she said she didn't think her head or chest hurt anymore. But later that afternoon, Franchion wrote Mom "isn't responding too well when I ask her if she has any pain, etc."

Marvel stayed with her that night. Mom slept in her recliner in the living room. Marvel noted she "was crooked in her chair at midnight so went to straighten her out. Kind of awake. Restless... Then she started breathing very loud."

February 12, 2015

Marvel jotted down Mom was awake, feeling better, and more alert that morning, but only for a few brief moments at a time.

When Darrell and I arrived shortly after noon, Mom was in a cold sweat. Her robe, chair, chair-liner, and her hair were all soaked with sweat. I noted her urine was tea-colored.

At 2:30, Mom appeared to be sleeping when she very clearly said, "I'm so hard of hearing." She woke at 4:30 and drank a little soda and water. I couldn't understand what she tried to say. She didn't seem to want to open her eyes.

I asked her if I could get her anything. She said no. It startled her when I'd talk to her— her eyes would open wide, then close again.

That evening at 5:00, Marvel, Steve, and Shonnie came. We noticed Mom seemed to grimace as if she was in pain, but when I asked her if she was, she said no.

Darrell and Steve moved Mom's hospital bed back into the living room. Mom was unable to walk at all that night. Marvel, Shonnie, and I got her from her recliner to the commode, to her bed. Since she fell asleep immediately after that, I jotted in the notebook, "No meds tonight."

February 13, 2015

Mom was having difficulty with her breathing. This is how I described it at 5:00 that morning: "Breathing heavy, then pauses, breathes again, then later more like puffs." At 7:00, after she rolled over onto her side, her breathing was more normal. I noted Mom had not taken any medication for her asthma for two days.

The nurse arrived at 9:45. She explained it was not asthma, it was cancer at that point and to treat the pain and labored breathing with morphine about every four hours. I paper-clipped a separate page to the back of the notebook for us to keep track of Mom's morphine doses and each medicine we gave her.

Since Mom was no longer receiving medications for her heart, the nurse warned us she could have a heart episode, an attack, or it may stop, and/or she could suffer an aortic aneurysm due to cancer. As disturbing as it was to think about those possibilities, it was better to be prepared.

Mom grimaced with pain every time she was moved during her bath that day. I made a note, "Always give her morphine twenty minutes before a bath." We also learned that using tabbed adult diapers was much easier on Mom than the pull-up type.

Mom was somewhat awake that afternoon. She could

see me and say my name. She smiled a bit when she tried to tell me about a "light." She said, "I'm so tired." I took off her glasses because she wanted them off. However, when I reached to remove her hearing aids, she stopped me and said, "I want to hear them when they come."

Bill and Linda, and Shonnie and Art came later. Like we did every evening (and as we had done with Dad), whoever was there would surround Mom's bed. We would recite our prayers together, express our love, and say our goodnights.

February 19, 2015

"Happy Valentine's Day!" was the first entry in the notebook. A yellow rose had been delivered with Meals on Wheels yesterday (because 02/14/2015 was a Saturday) as a gift for Mom; so lovely.

It was wonderful to see Mom smiling a lot that morning. She teasingly told me not to smile so much. I replied, "But you're so cute!" She smiled.

Later Mom's eyes were open, watery, and glassy while she appeared to be sleeping. She would startle when I approached her.

At 11:30, she tried to swallow a few sips of soda. It just wouldn't go down without Mom experiencing a lot of discomfort. When I offered her something for the pain, she refused it.

I set Sugarfoot on Mom's bed that afternoon. Mom smiled and kept clearly repeating, "Sugarfoot" (not "White Hook") as she stroked her much-adored kitty.

Peter and Jessie, and Marvel and Steve came later. Mom roused slightly to acknowledge them.

February 15, 2015

Mom woke at 5:30 a.m. and drank a little soda without showing any signs of pain. She smiled at me, wanted to hold my hand, and kiss me a lot. Sadly, I couldn't understand her words.

She did not want to let go of my hand. I wrote, "Not sleeping soundly, wants to hold my hand. Let her hold it 'til my hand was 'sleeping.' Laid her back to maybe sleep more soundly." Mom was restless.

At 7:00, she called out "Aubrey" over and over and kept talking. I heard her say something about "expecting." Mom kept repeating, "Expecting." I asked her if she was expecting someone; she said no. I asked her if someone was expecting her; she said yes.

Then Mom surprised me with how quickly her focus changed. I watched her eyes clearly follow something move across the living room floor. She couldn't tell me who or what it was. I mentioned "Virginia." Mom definitely did not want to talk about her or her mom and dad. It was 8:00 when Mom said she wanted to sleep.

By 8:15, I noticed her eyes open again. She looked at me and said, "I'm trying to figure something out." But Mom couldn't tell me what. She dozed for a couple of hours.

It was 10:15 when Mom's eyes were open but unfocused. She said "daughter" in such a way as to be making an introduction. Was Mom introducing me to someone?

Astonishingly Mom then raised her left hand high and slightly to the left. She smiled, looked at me, and said, "Oh, I guess I can't open the curtain." She lowered her hand.

An hour later, Mom said, "I can't wait 'til everything is quiet." Our puppy, Ellie, and Sugarfoot needed to be separated while in Mom's house. It was awful to hear Ellie barking when we needed to put her in a crate to keep her away from Sugarfoot. And it was just as annoying to hear Sugarfoot meowing when she was put in the basement to keep her away from Ellie. I could not find a workable solution to achieve a quiet, peaceful environment for Mom. I always felt bad about that.

Mom's attention quickly switched back to something (the curtain?). She said, "Every once in a while, I get a view." She couldn't tell me of what.

Shonnie came that afternoon. She also noted when Mom appeared to be sleeping, her eyes remained open. Shonnie told Mom she was talking to Bill on the phone. Mom said, "Hi, Bill." Then she slept soundly.

February 16, 2015

Shonnie saw Mom's arms were uncovered and that she felt cold at 12:45 a.m. When she was getting the blankets over Mom's arms, Mom said, "Wait 'til everyone gets here." Shonnie asked her if she'd like her hearing aids out. Mom said no.

At 6:20, Mom was awake and complaining about feeling sweaty and having pain around her abdomen. Shonnie gave her a small dose of morphine. Mom was able to say Shonnie's name.

After Franchion arrived, she noticed Mom was taking quick, shallow breaths. Her eyes were open and staring at the ceiling. She was talking very softly; Franchion couldn't understand what she was saying.

Then Mom reached out with her hand. Franchion took it and told Mom she'd be staying with her for a few days and that Shonnie and Marvel were at work, but they would be back later. After they said I love you to each other, Mom told Franchion she was going to try to sleep.

She rolled onto her side and asked, "Are you ready to go to church?" Mom rolled onto her back again and said something about "expecting Bill."

Franchion described how Mom folded her hands as if to pray. She moaned a little, so Franchion gave her some morphine with a sip of soda. Swallowing made Mom grimace. She dozed off.

Mom started to say something as she was moving her arms up and away from the bed. Mom clearly asked, "Do they want me to?" She started talking about church again. Franchion noted what Mom said, "I should go right now and see if they're open and ask them." She said more, but Franchion couldn't make out what it was.

Franchion jotted down (when she could understand again) that Mom asked if "someone was behind her, who it was, [then] motioning with [her] hands saying something about 'opening' but didn't mean the drapes. Mom was picking at her collar, resting, but with her eyes open and staring at the ceiling."

After I phoned later that morning, Franchion wrote, "[Mom] Said, 'Hi' to Malia, got teary, asked me if they were home. I said yes and with their dogs. Then Mom smiled and puckered her lips for Franchion to put balm on them before she closed her eyes."

When Diane came, Mom smiled and said, "Oh my gosh." Franchion and Mom talked with Diane about the church and something Mom was trying to say about "funeral." Diane asked Mom when the funeral would be. Mom replied, "Tomorrow." Mom told Diane she was afraid and she wanted to see her pastor. But then Mom said she knew the kids would take care of everything. She told Diane she just needed reassurance from the pastor to feel better. Then Mom looked up and said, "The lights are moving so fast."

Mom got teary-eyed when she said goodbye to Diane. Always before, when Diane was leaving, Mom would say, "See you next time."

Having been such an emotional visit, Franchion and Diane were crying at the breakfast counter when they noticed Sugarfoot had jumped onto Mom's bed. Sugarfoot moved close to Mom's face and reached out her paw to touch Mom. Mom said, "Oh, I'm not going to be here."

Diane called the church office and explained how things were with Mom. Pastor Wessel said he'd be there at 1:00.

When he walked into the living room, Mom smiled, took his hand (which she held throughout the visit), and told him how glad she was to see him. She asked him to say prayers with her. Mom told him she felt so much better and thanked him for coming.

The pastor told her he would come again. Mom asked him if it would be the next day; he told her yes. She wanted to know what time he would be there; he said about nine o'clock.

Franchion wrote that during his visit, Pastor Wessel "told Mom that both she and Dad were wonderful children of God, how she would see and be with Jesus and Dad in heaven, and that they would be able to *dance together again*."

Shonnie stopped in to visit Mom and Franchion when Mom said she was not in any pain before falling soundly asleep for that entire night.

February 17, 2015

Mom smiled and again announced she was not in any pain when Marvel stopped in before going to work. Franchion noted Mom said something about "meeting someone" and then the word "birthday." Franchion assumed Mom was remembering her ninety-first birthday; Franchion wrote, "I told her we were all together on her birthday and that we had such a good time, and she looked so pretty that she had shrimp and a Pink Squirrel. [Mom] said yes and smiled."

Mom asked what time it was and if she was in bed. Franchion told her the time and that, yes, she was in bed. Then Mom clearly and happily said, "They're coming to my house, and we're all going to fly together." After that, she closed her eyes.

When Aunt Aubrey arrived that afternoon, Mom looked at her and was able to voice, "Aubrey," as they held hands. Franchion called Uncle Alvin to let him know Mom was failing. He said that was too bad and he was sorry. He told us to do the best we all can and to call him "when it happens."

After the nurse got there and checked Mom, she again made us aware that Mom could have another stroke or become non-responsive. She told us how important it was to continue talking to Mom and to keep touching her. The nurse reminded us to change Mom's position often to avoid bed sores.

Franchion was writing in the notebook when she heard one loud and strange meow from Sugarfoot. She found her in Mom's bedroom, sitting in a corner. Franchion brought her out for a little food. She ate some, then immediately returned to the bedroom. This time she sat in the middle of the room.

Franchion wrote that "today [Sugarfoot] so wanted to be up on Mom's bed. At one point, Mom kind of opened her eyes, and I lifted Sugarfoot up [from the floor]. Mom smiled and reached out, so I put her on the bed so Mom could touch her, and Mom said, 'Sugarfoot.'"

Pastor Wessel stopped in that evening at 6:30; he apologized for not getting there earlier. He also told Franchion he would not be able to come the next day (because he would be giving two Ash Wednesday services), so he would plan to come Thursday.

Franchion told him Mom seemed more at peace—as if she could now rest—after his visit the day before. She also told him if he was able to stop on Thursday, even if Mom could only briefly open her eyes to see he was there, she was sure it would make Mom feel better.

At 8:30, Franchion had Mom ready to sleep for the

night. She said prayers; Mom was only able to say a couple of words. Franchion told her we all loved her very much. Mom smiled and reached out her hand.

Franchion wrote, "I held her hand and stroked her cheek (it was so soft and smooth). I said it was time to go to bed, night-night time. She said, 'Na-Na.'"

February 18, 2015

Mom slept through the night even though Franchion changed her position twice and noticed her breathing sounded "hollow" at times. Franchion described it as sounding like breathing "through a pipe or tube."

Marvel stopped in briefly on her way to work. Mom slightly woke, smiled, and was able to say "good morning" to both of them.

The nurse came at 11:30. After checking Mom, he informed Franchion he thought it would be days before Mom would die. He turned his attention to Mom; Franchion noted the exchange, "He said, 'You look as cute as ever.' She said yes and smiled."

One of Mom's closest friends came that day. Mom recognized her but could not speak. Her friend sat next to Mom and talked to her. Franchion jotted, "Emotional."

Later Clay and Maija arrived. Mom opened her eyes, smiled, and said, "Hi." Franchion wrote: "[Mom] became more alert with eyes open and responding, saw Clay had on Grandpa's checkerboard shirt and shook [her] head yes when he mentioned it."

Marvel came during Clay and Maija's visit. Franchion continued, "Marvel held up Sugarfoot for [Mom] to see, and she really smiled. Clay and Maija said goodbye. She was trying to say something to Clay, [he] couldn't understand, but [Mom] smiled."

After Clay, Maija, and Franchion left, Marvel noted another friend of Mom's called at 7:00. She added that Mom slept through the night and that her breathing was "loud and steady and regular."

February 19, 2015

That morning, Franchion at 7:35, Shonnie at 10:20, and Diane at 11:00, all called to check on Mom. Marvel explained that Mom apparently did not want her mouth swabbed since she clenched her teeth and then went right back to sleep. After describing Mom's condition to Diane, Diane told Marvel things seemed to be progressing normally.

Marvel left after Darrell and I (with our dogs, Lambeau and Ellie) arrived shortly after noon. Mom's eyes blinked to let us know she heard us. She continued to breathe heavily with her eyes slightly open, glassy and watery. Her cheeks felt cool, but her hands were warm.

After I saw the distinct purple patches on both Mom's feet at 3:15, I called my siblings. Now we were all very aware that Mom would be leaving us soon. Shonnie, Marvel, and Steve were at Mom's house by 5:00 that evening. Marvel gave Mom morphine at 5:41, and I gave her another dose at 7:16. Franchion and Keith arrived at 8:15. I noted Mom moaned at times that night.

February 20, 2015

At 12:05 a.m., Mom made a loud cough. Art came shortly after that, and Bill was with us by 2:30. Marvel and Steve, Art, and Keith left, and Darrell went to bed not too long after Bill got there. Shonnie, Franchion, Bill, and I stayed up through the night talking and enjoying reminiscing with each other. Mom let us know she was listening by clearing her throat once at 3:38 that morning.

The nurse arrived at 11:15 to check on Mom. She thought Mom had hours to live.

Mom's Final Moments

Marvel, Franchion, Shonnie, Bill, and I were gathered around Mom's bed. Steve, Darrell, and Art were sitting nearby. We were all grappling with our intense emotions. It was so difficult knowing it was actually happening. Mom was leaving us.

At 4:50 p.m., we thought Mom was going; I heard us saying, "She's gonna go!"—but she took another breath. A few minutes later, we repeated, "She's gonna go." Again, she took another breath. There was a remarkable change at 5:10. Art commented, "Being a cop, I've seen a lot of guys die, and she *is* gonna go." We laughed as we were weeping.

At 5:15, as Mom did draw her final breath, her eyes marvelously opened wide. They became "alive" with an almost jewel-like crystalline and brilliant blue color, stunningly beautiful! I believe she was at last allowed to fully open the curtain, she was being welcomed into heaven by angels, and she could see Him, in all His glory, with open arms reaching out to embrace her!

February 20, 2015, Continued

We phoned the nurse; she arrived at 6:30 p.m. to officially pronounce Mom dead. Maureen and Trenton of Anderson Funeral Home came and took Mom's body fifteen minutes later. I remember it feeling as if time had completely lapsed... *Hadn't we just mourned Dad's body being taken away?*

February 21, 2015

That morning I washed Mom's robe, bedding, and linens while Darrell vacuumed the carpeting. Franchion and Keith, Bill, and Shonnie came. We chose three appropriate and lovely Bible verses for Mom's funeral service. Then we noticed Sugarfoot was lying on the head of Mom's bed obviously grieving. She did not do her usual purr when we pet her. It was very painful to see her missing her "mom" so much.

We went to Anderson Funeral Home at one o'clock to make final funeral arrangements with Maureen and to view Mom. She looked so beautiful and so peaceful.

After returning to the house, we had a discussion on how we might start sorting Mom and Dad's things. Later, Bill went home, and the rest of us met Art, Marvel, and Steve at the same supper club where only twenty-eight days earlier we had celebrated Mom's birthday. I noted, "We had a great time celebrating the life that Mom and Dad had shared."

February 22, 2015

Aunt Aubrey, Marvel and Steve, Franchion and Keith, Darrell and I, and Shonnie met at the funeral home to see Mom for the last time. I signed the cremation form.

Back at Mom and Dad's house, we furthered the discussion on how to begin the enormous task of sorting Mom and Dad's things. Franchion and Keith took Sugarfoot home to live with them.

That evening Darrell and I went to Marvel and Steve's for a little while before returning to Mom and Dad's house... where Mom and Dad no longer lived.

February 23, 2015

I wrote in the notebook that "Mom's hospital bed, bed-side table, commode, and wheelchair ramp were picked up at 12:30. Shonnie ordered flowers. Marvel, Shonnie, Bill, and I went through some boxes in the basement. *Whew!*" We were discovering that Mom and Dad had saved (almost) everything!

February 29, 2015

It was a quiet day at Mom and Dad's house. Only Darrell and I were there. We watched the video of their fiftieth wedding anniversary celebration. Later we went to Marvel and Steve's. It was my birthday.

February 25, 2015

Mom's visitation was held that evening between four and eight o'clock at Anderson Funeral Home. Maureen and Trenton once again welcomed us into an exquisitely prepared gathering room. Even though it was very cold (just eight degrees above zero), the large number of people who came warmed our hearts tremendously.

February 26, 2015

We met at Grace Lutheran Church at ten o'clock for a brief visitation before Mom's eleven o'clock funeral service. I remember how magnificently the shapes in the stained glass windows came to life from the sunlight pouring through them.

Approximately ninety people attended on that clear, brilliant, and extremely cold winter day. At the graveside part of the service, I was very concerned for Pastor Wessel's hands as he read from his notes. He had forgotten to bring gloves!

Maureen dropped off the flowers and plants from the service for us to continue to enjoy at Mom and Dad's house. I wrote, "I canceled [Mom's] cell phone and her home phone" at four o'clock that afternoon.

February 27, 2015

I noted that I canceled Mom's TV subscription.

The notebook entries for Mom ended

We had no idea what Mom and Dad had chosen for their tombstone or how it would be inscribed until it was placed on their gravesite.

Between their names, they honored their union:

Married

June 21

1947

Below that, they honored each of us:

Parents of

Marvel, Franchion, Malia, Shonnie, William K

About the Author

Malia was the bookkeeper for her dad's feed and farm supply store while living and working on a dairy farm in rural Wisconsin, followed by living and working on a cattle ranch in Montana. Twenty-four years after high school graduation, she attended the University of Wisconsin, Madison. Within four years, she received a bachelor of arts with honors in sociology. During her senior year, she was one of four runners-up for the Outstanding Undergraduate Returning Adult Student Award. Malia is also a semi-retired ballroom dance studio owner and instructor who lives full-time in an RV with her husband, Darrell Shelby, and their two dogs, Ellie and Shelby.